SALEM COLLEGE
LIBRARY

The Archie K. Davis
Collection of
Southern History & Literature

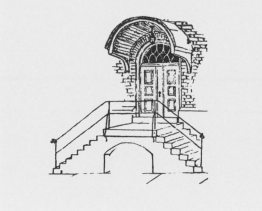

The Fiction of
Ellen Gilchrist

The Fiction of
Ellen Gilchrist
An Appreciation

Brad Hooper

 PRAEGER

Westport, Connecticut
London

Library of Congress Cataloging-in-Publication Data

Hooper, Brad
   The Fiction of Ellen Gilchrist : an appreciation / Brad Hooper.
     p. cm.
   Includes bibliographical references and index.
   ISBN 0–275–98593–8 (alk. paper)
   1. Gilchrist, Ellen, 1935—Criticism and interpretation. 2. Women and literature—
United States—History—20th century. I. Title.
  PS3557.I34258Z68   2005
  813'.54—dc22   2004028070

British Library Cataloguing in Publication Data is available.

Library of Congress Catalog Card Number: 2004028070
ISBN: 0–275–98593–8

First published in 2005

Praeger Publishers, 88 Post Road West, Westport, CT 06881
An imprint of Greenwood Publishing Group, Inc.
www.praeger.com

Printed in the United States of America

∞™

The paper used in this book complies with the
Permanent Paper Standard issued by the National
Information Standards Organization (Z39.48–1984).

10 9 8 7 6 5 4 3 2 1

*This book, a labor of love, is dedicated to my parents,
William and Elizabeth Hooper, of Charleston, Illinois,
for their continued belief in everything I do.
And to the staff of* Booklist *magazine at the American Library
Association—my professional "family"—for such spirited and
meaningful support of this project; in particular,* Booklist
*editor-in-chief Bill Ott for granting me a sabbatical leave to finish it.
And to Brendan Driscoll, buddy and muse, whose encouraging
voice I heard in my ear as I wrote every sentence.*

Contents

Chapter 1

An Introduction

A FRIEND AND I, after attending a national conference of librarians held in New Orleans in January 1998, took a five-day car trip to the Louisiana plantation country and then up into Mississippi. Our primary destination was Natchez, where we would spend most of our time. I have an abiding interest in southern history and literature, perhaps a product of early environmental influence, since my birthplace was Vandalia, Illinois, which actually is located south of what would be a continuation of the Mason Dixon Line if drawn farther westward. Vandalia (the second capital of the state; Springfield, the current one, is the third town to hold that distinction) lies nestled nearly forgotten in southern Illinois, which topographically and even culturally, linguistically, and historically has ties to the upper South, as if the blue Ohio simply did not exist as a geographical division between North and South.

Given my interest in southern culture, Natchez had for years been on my list of necessary places to visit; and now I had the opportunity. By population, as I quickly learned during the travel planning stage, Natchez ranks as only a middle-size town in today's world, not a city at all; its historical significance, of course, extends well beyond its modest population. My traveling companion and I left New Orleans in early afternoon; we approached Natchez from the southeast, driving through the cool, clear January dusk, through lush, dark green pine forests. The car engine purred as we negotiated the road's slight rises and descents, drawing nearer to the town and, as if by the gravitational pull, to the great river itself. We entered the city limits just after nightfall and headed to the central business district, to the venerable hotel where we had made a reservation—a hotel enjoying a guidebook-supported national reputation. Before actually being able to pull into the hotel parking lot, one-way streets necessitated our circling around. But that minor inconvenience provided us with an unanticipated delight: the sight of what we hadn't intended to actually see this evening or even to necessarily see *at night*. The crown jewel of Natchez's surviving antebellum mansions. With floodlights bringing its elegant, columned, neoclassic facade out of the darkness, it struck the chord—as of an overture—we had come to Natchez to hear and feel: the chord of the Old South.

What is *today* in every other place is still *the day before yesterday* in Natchez—which is not to suggest that the contemporary ways of racial thinking in Natchez correspond to the attitudes of days long gone. But the physical place, the "furniture" of the town, in large part remains close to the original form. Natchez flourished in its day as an opulent center for wealthy southern planters, supported in their luxury by vast land holdings, not only in Mississippi, but also across the river in Louisiana. They gathered in Natchez to build town residences reflecting their material success. The result, for us today, is a town that is an outdoor museum, a place of incredible historical artifacts: not tools and scraps of clothing, but fully intact houses.

So, as early as possible the next morning, my traveling partner and I walked the few blocks from our hotel to the lovely house we had seen so beautifully illuminated the evening before. With its grounds, it occupies an entire city block, the house itself sitting atop a small rise, thus its magnificence—its preeminence over all the Natchez mansions—announced for all to hear. Its size is impressive, but no less striking is its beauty of line and detail. It doesn't simply bespeak—but *shouts*—the gracious living that was conducted under its roof many, many decades ago. (Of course, one must never lose sight of the fact that such a living had its basis in the cotton industry, which was itself based on slave labor.)

We asked for a tour of the house and were gladly accorded one. This was not a particularly heavy period in the tourist season (*perfect* weather, though, for me from the cold Midwest: highs on our trip in the 50s and 60s); so the two of us got a docent all to ourselves. A Mississippi accent is to me the most infectious accent there is; within two minutes of hearing one, I want to speak like a native Mississippian, too, but refrain as best I can from falling into imitating it, for fear my inauthenticity will not only come through but also strike the true Mississippian as mocking.

The docent assigned to us spoke beautiful Mississippian, and she looked as lovely and gracious as the house in which we stood. No strand of her glowing silver hair loosened and drooped away from the elegant French roll into which it had been folded. True, the shoes looked a little too "comfy," but excusably so, given her duties here. Her skirt and sweater were obviously finely woven and tailored, in a dark shade of plum—the result of her keen awareness of the color choices that best showed off her striking hair.

"Where y'all from?" she inquired of us as she took her first step down the front hall to show us the spacious, heavily decorated first-floor rooms.

"Chicago." "New York."

The possibility that her narrative might need to be altered for us registered on her face as the briefest of shutters; and, too, there was a short hesitation in her step—not really a stumble, but as if she'd subtly rescued herself from one. Not until a few minutes had passed when she paused in her history of the house before uttering the word "Yankee," did we actually realize the reason for her brief falter upon learning where we were from. But when she got "Yankee" out, we smiled our acceptance of hearing it—our way of reassuring her that she had had no reason to worry about making any adjustments in her memorized commentary.

After a generous, informative viewing of the first floor (but with the lingering question on our minds, how in voluminous nineteenth-century clothing did people tolerate the hot Mississippi summers?), we were guided to the second floor. No room was locked against the tourist's eye, and the bedrooms here on the second floor gave us a picture of less formal life led under this roof. Our docent drew us to the back of the wide central hall dividing this floor from front to back, just as a wide corridor also separated the rooms on the floor beneath—the halls' width explained to us as purposeful in keeping the house's interior as open to refreshing breezes as possible—and from this elevation at the rear of the house we could peer down into the rear gardens, directly into a very modern swimming pool. No old brick-lined pond for water lilies and goldfish; most definitely a modern pool for swimming in and sunning beside.

"A pool," my traveling companion said, verbalizing the obvious; but, just as obviously, he was wanting some information about it. To encourage the docent, then, which indeed it *did* do, he added, "Was it put in when the house was a private girls' school?" (In her downstairs introduction she had chronicled for us the various incarnations the house had gone through after private ownership had come to an end soon after the Civil War.)

Her words came delivered in exquisite but emphatic politeness. "No, it was installed by the ladies of the Garden Club." (Another fact previously given to us: that the premises were currently owned and operated by the Garden Club of Natchez.)

My companion persisted, to what end other than simple annoyance I could not venture a guess. "For public use?"

The docent went more rigid and cocked her head. "I beg your pardon?"

"For use by the townspeople?"

She stepped closer to him. Her voice emerged lower but sharper: like a good opera singer's losing none of its clarity when dipping into a lower range. "I said it was for the ladies of the Garden Club."

"Only for the Club's use?"

She took yet another step forward toward my companion, provocatively leaving only a foot of electrified air separating them. "I really don't want to have to tell you again. It is for the ladies of the Garden Club."

Give it up, I silently pleaded with my companion, which, fortunately, he did. Fortunately, too, the tour had come to its planned finishing point. We beat a rather hasty retreat, our docent's smile, which remained as frozen on her face as this part of the state of Mississippi *never* gets, being the last thing we saw as we turned and ran. Back in the car, I asked my companion if he had been trying to provoke an actual face-slap. No, he answered; he insisted that he truly hadn't realized how offended she'd gotten till the very end. "Basically, I was just making conversation, just letting her know we were definitely paying attention to her and interested in the house and what she had to tell us about it."

Then we laughed. We didn't laugh *at* the situation and certainly not *at* our docent. We laughed over how beautifully such an incident had arrived into our hands: a perfect example of human nature acting out when propriety is at stake, when someone's idea of the proper order of things is questioned, when *privilege* is questioned. I am confident that Ellen Gilchrist, herself a native Mississippian, would also have found this incident amusing. With the marvelous sense of humor she displays in her fiction, I cannot imagine she could resist finding humor in this situation. She undoubtedly would appreciate it for more than its human nature value because it is about the ways of the Old South left over in the New South, about how social isolationism can lead to a collective, communal, conservative way of seeing how the social order should be arranged, despite a more progressive world existing in the outside world. For instance, read her novella "The Cabal" in the collection *The Cabal and Other Stories,* to enjoy her take on social privilege under attack by a new and frightening force. (Of course, I will be discussing this work at its proper place in the course of this appreciation.)

Sarah Conley, the eponymous main character of Gilchrist's sixth novel, offers this musing: "Writing a book. The real thing. The thing that hurts and scares you and makes you laugh and makes you learn and be challenged."[1] At a later point Sarah posits, "Every writer gets to take a chance on writing their book. What the hell, it's the big reward."[2] I can only concur that writing a book is both challenging and rewarding. My reward was having read all of Gilchrist's fictional prose. And I count myself fortunate, for how many people can honestly say, upon putting down the last of an author's books, that they retain all their interest in and admiration for that author? As I approached the writing of this book, I could only underscore Gilchrist's own sentiment about tackling new projects as expressed in her *Journals*: "The day I no longer do anything that frightens me and makes me shy I will know I am finished as a writer."[3] As I proceeded into and through the preparation of this book, I shared another of her sentiments: "The reason to write is to learn. The more I write, the more I am forced to learn."[4]

This book is, plainly, a critical appreciation of Ellen Gilchrist's novels and short story collections as they are to be taken at face value; in other words, I draw no parallels and connections between the author's life and her work. I presume no intentionality on her part; I only read what is given and guess not or assess not what might be the author's intention beyond the offering of a work of fiction to be appreciated and estimated for only what it is and not for what it is supposed to be or can be or will be. I salute the late, great Canadian novelist Carol Shields, who, in her life of Jane Austen, said, even though her book is indeed a biography, "This is, in the end, what matters: the novels themselves, and not the day-to-day life of the author, the cream cakes she bought at a bakery."[5]

Themes to be explored—the thematic threads I will pursue throughout the course of this critical survey—are set out in the first chapter as I examine Gilchrist's first short story collection. The book bridges, I hope, the worlds of reviewing and criticism, blending the immediacy of reaction that is characteristic of the former and the more sober, more specifically focused second and third look that defines the latter.

Of course a biographical and career profile will prove helpful as background, especially to readers turning to this book without extensive experience reading her works. Ellen Louise Gilchrist was born in Natchez,

Mississippi, on February 20, 1935, the second child of a professional basketball player-turned-engineer. Much of her early life was spent on the Hopedale Plantation in Vicksburg, her maternal grandfather's home.[6] In her childhood, during World War II, her family relocated to Harrisburg, Illinois, her father sent there through his involvement in domestic, home-front war work. Gilchrist was not especially keen on attending school, but she nevertheless read "voraciously."[7] Her first marriage was contracted when she was in her late teens: an elopement, in fact, and not a particularly happy marriage, "with frequent separations."[8] Three sons and a sequence of marriages followed.

At age 32, she obtained a BA in philosophy from Millsaps College in Jackson, Mississippi.[9] Her writing career did not actually begin until she had passed her fortieth year. In the late 1970s, she served as a contributing editor for the *Vieux Carre Courier*, a New Orleans newspaper.[10] In 1976 she was invited by writer Jim Whitehead to attend the creative writing program he cofounded at the University of Arkansas. While there, in 1979, she published a volume of poetry called *The Land Surveyor's Daughter*; also in that year she won a National Endowment Grant to write a volume of stories.[11] In 1981 this collection was published by the University of Arkansas Press under the title *In the Land of Dreamy Dreams,* which garnered considerable acclaim, and the first edition sold out, with the rights subsequently picked up by Little, Brown, who published a second edition, and has remained her publisher. Later she published another volume of poetry (1986), *Riding out the Tropical Depression: Selected Poems, 1975–1985;* but it is, of course, as a fiction writer that her name has been made. Public exposure to her storytelling was increased when, in 1984, she began a short stint on National Public Radio's "Morning Edition" show; her radio pieces were eventually gathered into book form in the previously cited *Falling through Space: the Journals of Ellen Gilchrist* (1987).[12] In 1983 she published her first novel, *The Annunciation,* which was quickly followed by the story collection *Victory over Japan* (1984), which won the National Book Award. Her sequence of fiction titles, 18 by 2004, has been published on a regular basis since then, alternating between novels and short story collections. The appearance in 2000 of her *Collected Stories* heralded an "arrival": a recognition of her established place in the contemporary American short story scene. And the publication of a short story collection subsequent to the *Collected Stories* is a statement to her plans to continue at full-steam, at least as a short story writer, obviously with no "retirement" in mind after the *Collected Stories* looked back over her career in the form.

Gilchrist has won several awards in addition to the National Book Award. These include a Mississippi Arts Festival poetry award in 1968, a *New York Quarterly* award for poetry in 1978, the previously mentioned National Endowment for the Arts grant in 1979, a *Prairie Schooner* award in 1981, a Mississippi Academy award in 1982, and a University of Arkansas Fulbright award in 1985.[13] She is currently on the faculty of the University of Arkansas in Fayetteville, and she maintains homes there and in Ocean Springs, Mississippi.

Critically, Gilchrist is still thought of as primarily a short story writer, despite some notable successes as a novelist. And in both critics' minds and in the popular consciousness, she is best known for her feisty, independent female characters—especially highly regarded are her recurrent female characters, a gallery, a "stable," if you will—that had come to include Rhoda Manning, Nora Jane Whittington, Crystal Manning, her maid Traceleen, and Anna Hand.

Ostensibly Gilchrist is a writer of the New South, investigating in her fiction very contemporary social issues, such as the evolving social roles of women, family restraints and restrictions on the individual, racism, divorce, abortion, drug use, and promiscuity in the face of viral terror—but always refracting these issues through the prism of Old South notions of the importance of family and place and social propriety.

But one aspect of Gilchrist as a fiction writer is deeply and *completely* grounded in Old South cultural traditions, which she has inherited from southern writers of generations before her: her voice; her "yarny" eloquence, in which resonates the strong oral tradition found in most southern writing. The "front porch" factor, as it were: the voice that narrates southern fiction being the same voice that relates local gossip on long summer evenings in the Delta. Examples will be shared throughout the pages that follow.

So now, on to her stories and novels, to appreciate her distinction.

Chapter 2

Gilchrist's Short Story Debut
(*In the Land of Dreamy Dreams*)

ELLEN GILCHRIST'S FIRST BOOK of fiction was a collection of short stories called *In the Land of Dreamy Dreams* (only the first of many intriguing, provocative titles with which she would christen her books). It gathered 14 stories, five previously published in such well-regarded literary journals as *Prairie Schooner* and *New Orleans Review,* and it made its distinguished appearance in 1981.

In the Land of Dreamy Dreams is an exceptionally strong book of fiction, especially for a *first* book of fiction. It received significant critical and popular attention, which it has continued to garner, explaining its continued in-print status. For instance, Jim Crace, a British novelist quite popular and well regarded these days, said in *The Times Literary Supplement* that the book is "a sustained display of delicately and rhythmically modulated prose, and an unsentimental dissection of raw sentiment. Her stories are perceptive; her manner is both stylish and idiomatic—a rare and potent combination."[1] The book is undoubtedly fine entertainment. By this first book of fiction, Gilchrist established that she is capable of writing artfully and entertainingly at the same time, a dual appeal that continues to be appreciated by critics and general readers equally. Jeanie Thompson and Anita Miller Garner, in their essay "The Miracle of Realism: The Bid for Self-Knowledge in the Fiction of Ellen Gilchrist," which appeared in *The Southern Quarterly,* and is frequently cited in critical discussions about Gilchrist, maintain that "Few writers can achieve with a first collection of short stories published by a university press the kind of instant popular success and critical acclaim Ellen Gilchrist won with *In the Land of Dreamy Dreams*"; and that she "captures the flavor and essence of her region without drowning in its idiom. She does not diminish her work by parroting already established Southern voices or depending upon stereotypes of landscape and character."[2]

If for some reason Gilchrist had never written another book after *Dreamy Dreams,* or, if she had turned to writing novels exclusively, and this collection came to represent her only activity in the field of the short story, *Dreamy Dreams* would still be a testament to her gifts in this field and remembered for its craft. It announced the arrival of a new fiction writer—particularly a new short story writer—to be reckoned with. It set a high-water mark for her; it is the book by which all her subsequent ones have been judged, for better or worse.

But of course, dissent about any book generally published to acclaim is inevitable, and one such negative estimation of *Dreamy Dreams* is found in Dorie LaRue's essay "Progress and Prescription: Ellen Gilchrist's Southern Belles," which also appeared in *The Southern Quarterly,* in which she insists that "In her first collection of short stories . . . female protagonists such as Rhoda, Matile, Alisha, and Amanda are guided exclusively by their desires, lusts, greed and rebellious natures . . . and they all seem to be caught in some arrested stage of character development."[3]

But for our purposes here, *Dreamy Dreams* serves well as an introduction to the major elements and qualities of Gilchrist's fiction that add up to her distinction and excellence; by their identification in *Dreamy Dreams,* I will outline the themes we will pursue through all of her work.

Even before delving into the stories individually, let us establish that the foremost feature of her fiction, by which she has gained her fame and appreciation and for which she will continue to be read and analyzed, is her female characters. Specifically, how she depicts and develops female protagonists; what it is that individualizes *her* expression of the female consciousness and experience. (As Margaret B. McDowell remarks in her entry on Ellen Gilchrist in *Contemporary Novelists,* "The stories achieve distinction because of their concentration, intensity, and variety, and because of their authentic presentation of feminine protagonists, who are aggressive and ambitious to the point of becoming destructive or self-destructive, but who are also, to a degree, sympathetic figures, especially as children."[4]) A typical Gilchrist female character, then, is drawn as a celebrant of the independence of spirit and, further, the impulse toward defying convention regardless of consequences social or even legal. In her explorations of the female in an untrammeled state, Gilchrist goes mining, in particularly and most revealingly, the milieu she knows most about, the one into which she was born and raised: the white, upper-middle-class, southern world. She makes it a telling environment for investigation into traditional female roles and the results and ramifications of avoiding or shedding those roles. Her characters say "No." Society counters with a "Yes, indeed, Missy!" Some may falter and compromise with one leg standing in independence while keeping the other leg in tradition, that arena where women play it safe under masculine support and protection.

The landscape into which Gilchrist shines an often witty, occasionally sarcastic, but always sympathetic light includes the South of Gilchrist's upbringing, from the 1940s to the present day; the South burdened by remnants of the Old South, the New and more cosmopolitan South in full swing; and places outside the South where southerners may go but always take with them southern customs and idioms. She reveals an alternative truth about women bending, breaking, going around, or ducking expected roles; she is forthright about the end result of their pursuits in this direction: sometimes they are successful, other times they are thwarted by some outside force, or occasionally they are the victim of their own sabotage.

The great contribution of Ellen Gilchrist to American literature, announced initially to the world in her first book of fiction, the collection of stories *In the Land of Dreamy Dreams*, is the truth she reveals in her characters, primarily female ones, to have them test the constraints of their lives and goad them into discovering the maximal dimensions of their character.

In *Falling through Space: The Journals of Ellen Gilchrist*, she identifies the book by saying, "This is supposed to be a writer's journal and if there is one thing I've learned about writing it is to follow your compulsion."[5] Be true to yourself, in other words; write not only what you want to write, without regard for what others may expect you to write about, but express the *truth* as you see it about life and experiences and how you observe and understand them: which is how that comment from her *Journals* should be interpreted, and which is a maxim that has seen her through the writing of all her books. Basically, then, she has adhered to the principal that if you are honest with your reader, they will come. Her first book of fiction, *In the Land of Dreamy Dreams*, can be taken as a position paper on that philosophy; it can be seen as her first promise that honesty will be her guiding force in all her fiction.

The credibility of her characters—again, especially her female ones—is everywhere evident in this book. They are familiar to us: recognizable as ourselves, family members, friends, coworkers, people next door and down the street. Truthfulness in their psychology and behavior draws readers to them, comfortableness with them as real people eliciting empathy with their situations that apply to us all.

Gilchrist's honest, truthful female characters for the most part violate social strictures put in place to subdue women physically and emotionally. Keep in your traditional place, society warns these women. Her fiction, then, beginning with the short-story collection *In the Land of Dreamy Dreams*, tracks the ways in which women do *not* stay in place and shares the repercussions of their actions. She asks questions she wants her female protagonists to answer, primary among them, Does selfishness necessarily have to accompany a woman's independence? But also, is marital discord an automatic by-product? Certainly we see a lot of both in her fiction, when women take stands that are tantamount, by old traditional southern standards, to taking to the barricades in open rebellion.

First, we need to identify another element arising in her depiction of female characters: which is, they sometimes experience *ambivalence* about independence, about setting their own path, about shedding the protection of men. A very real state, of course, since people are not only one thing or the other; they are all things. People are a mixture of compulsions, attitudes, and emotions, some of which are, of course, conflicting. Few people are Joan-of-Arc-type personalities, single-minded and steadfast in following a freeing course of action regardless of the personal danger generated by their stand-taking.

Let us return for a moment to the pages of Gilchrist's journals *Falling through Space* and listen to her talk about men and her reaction to them, which is helpful in appreciating the ambivalence she often imparts to her otherwise independent-minded female protagonists: "There are many people who read my books and decide that I am a feminist," she observes. She disputes that. "I like men," she avers, as if holding that liking men is in and of itself proof against feminist tendencies. She goes on further to say that "I like men because they protect me. All my life they have protected me and I believe they will go on doing it as long as I love them in return."[6]

This from an author who has built a career writing about women who recoil from men's interference? Of course she has, and done it *honestly*, for it is this "man-lovingness" in her that gives her female characters the irony that in turn broadens them and leaves them compelling and *real*.

"Men want me to tell them how beautiful they are and how much we like the way their shoulders grow so wide and their arms so long and how we love their voices to be deep and how we like them to laugh at us and pretend we are dumber than they are," she admits in her *Journals*.[7] But she is not compromising herself as a woman by liking men, by doing for them what they like. For she gets just as much out of it: for her, the masculine presence like a fine scent and a warm coat. "I am an old-fashioned woman," she insists in her *Journals*,[8] which, however, does not prohibit her from looking into "new-fashioned" attitudes toward convention and men, seeing for herself where a new-fashioned path leads them; or how, as intriguingly, women "old-fashioned" in their domestic and social situations feel, whether yet conscious of it or not, the strains of nonconformity.

All this means that Gilchrist's female characters stand firm in their believability. She herself avowedly likes men and their protectiveness, and this viewpoint actually plays well in her fiction, for it tempers her depictions of women in conflict with traditional gender roles, saving her from the soapbox. Her fiction comes across not as a diatribe or a tract. It is about spunky individuals, plainly and simply. Whether we root for them in every situation or not, we can't walk away from them: which is the sheer essence of Gilchrist's writing genius.

Now, for a minute's backtracking. Previously I insisted that her first book of fiction, the story collection *In the Land of Dreamy Dreams*, serves as the perfect introduction to the outstanding qualities of Gilchrist's fiction; and the major one has been identified: the nature of her female protagonists. Let us now examine a second distinctive trait of her fiction, which, like the first, *Dreamy Dreams* fully displays. I mentioned it in the introductory chapter: her voice.

Gilchrist's is a yarn-spinning voice, a southern voice; but that latter descriptive is not an implication of a derivativeness. Gilchrist writes in the southern tradition of oral storytelling, with emphasis on family and place, but without hints of imitation of, say, William Faulkner or, even more significantly, since Gilchrist was a friend of hers, Eudora Welty. These two figures, Faulkner and Welty, reign even after their deaths as the supreme stylistic giants of southern literature, and it can not be helped that a contemporary writer who tries to echo either one of these unique voices will stand out, and annoyingly so, as imitative. (Reynolds Price, for example, seems to cleave closer and closer to Welty's style, to his detriment.)

But Gilchrist's limpid, sheer eloquence is her own. Her style is clean, lean, and clear. She maintains a wise but humorous "homespun" quality to her voice. Correlative to the realism of her characters, to her version of truthfulness in which she creates them, her voice is realistic and authentic. Her readability and popularity is explained by this match between the honesty of her characters and the authenticity of her voice.

Woven into her yarn-spinning voice is a delightful wit, both the rib-tickling and the sarcastic varieties. But she is never mean. Her humor is always the "laugh-with-you" not "laugh-at-you" type. Another impressive attribute of her style is how comfortably and relevantly she can slip into a beautifully effective metaphor that does not overwhelm the reader or the flow with over-rich, self-conscious language.

In the stories collected in *Dreamy Dreams* we encounter yet another important aspect of Gilchrist's fiction: her technique. How she structures her stories to exploit the strengths of the form itself to maximum effect—primarily, how she offers certain "slices" of a character in the flash-point way that characterizes what the short-story form can do best. As I mentioned in the introductory chapter, Gilchrist is generally thought of as a short-story writer over a novelist. Certainly her most famous book is the National Book Award–winning short story collection *Victory over Japan*. But regardless of popular image, is she actually, then, a better short story writer than novelist? That question will be explored throughout this appreciation.

In the Land of Dreamy Dreams will introduce two more traits of her fiction that go hand in hand. One is her swift, concise scene-setting and character description, by which she does *not* leave the reader with a sense that abbreviation is standing in for what should have been spelled out in more detail. The second is her good ear for dialogue and her use of it to reveal character.

Now, finally, to the stories themselves that comprise *In the Land of Dreamy Dreams*. These 14 stories are arranged into 3 groupings: "There is a Garden of Eden" (which is also the title of one of the stories in the group), "Things Like the Truth," and "Perils of the Nile" (this, too, the title of one of the group's stories). The stories in the first group are generally linked by characters attempting to find a place of inner peace. In the second group of stories, characters tend to encounter the brutal realities of life and human nature. And in the third group, juvenile characters must deal with the hurdles all people must face in growing up—in front of them are placed, often for the first time, adult concerns that, when dealt with, advance the young protagonist into adulthood.

The weakest stories in the book—there are four of these—are ironically all found in the second grouping. (None of these four was selected for inclusion in Gilchrist's *Collected Stories*, appearing in 2001.)

"Rich," the first story in the collection, is one of the collection's best, for it showcases the author's strengths. The meaning of the title is indicated in the opening line: "Tom and Letty Wilson were rich in everything."[9] In a mere eight words, Gilchrist establishes the salient characteristic of the lives of this married couple. She goes on to limn the world of the Wilsons, a milieu to which she will return many times in her probes of the faults and fallacies of social structure—and stricture. Tom, so this first paragraph informs, is a bank vice president in New Orleans, and his wife, Letty, is a vice president as well: of the Junior League, "her picture in *Town and Country* every year at the Symphony Ball."[10] More clues to her life and character are delivered in this passage: "Every year from Epiphany to Fat Tuesday they flew the beautiful green and gold and purple flag outside their house that meant that Letty had been queen of the Mardi Gras the year she was a debutante. Not that Letty was foolish enough to take the flag seriously."[11]

That last line is a quick first taste of Gilchrist's sarcastic pokes. Letty indeed takes the flag seriously; it flies on high as a social emblem, reminding people of her social standing in New Orleans society. A little further on is one of Gilchrist's quick but resonant thumbnail sketches—of Tom, in this case. She says about him: "Tom Wilson considered himself a natural as a banker because he loved to gamble and wheel and deal. From the time he was a boy in a small Baptist town in Tennessee he had loved to play cards and match nickels and lay bets."[12]

Again in her trademark succinctness, Gilchrist adds an additional side to Tom: that his "personality was too flamboyant for the conservative Whitney Bank, but he was cheerful and cooperative and when he made a mistake he had the ability to turn it into an anecdote."[13] Tom is indeed charming, but he is also superficial. He lacks substance: all talk and little action. These few pages of the story so far have established Gilchrist's aptitude for brief but indelible impressions of people, for painting the essentials of a character's appearance, general behavior, and place in their particular corner of the world. This adeptness will be repeatedly shown in her short stories: How quickly she can impart an understanding of characters' attitudes, personalities, and actions.

So, it was love at first sight for Letty. Tom had come to Tulane on a football scholarship, and his charm led to membership in a fraternity of rich boys from New Orleans. Letty's "plain sweet looks and expensive clothes excited him."[14] She came from a very good family, and her wedding to Tom was a big affair, "with twelve bridesmaids, four flower girls, and seven hundred guests. It was pronounced a marriage made in heaven, and Letty's mother ordered masses said in Rome for their happiness."[15]

But it is a new world Letty experiences on their honeymoon. "Tom's hands touching her seemed a strange and exciting passage that will carry her simple dreamy existence to a reality she had never encountered,"[16] and "before the day was out Letty became the first girl in her crowd to break the law of God and the Napoleonic Code by indulging in oral intercourse."[17]

The first five pages of the story are not really the "story" at all. They set the scene and fill readers in on the backstory. The social environment is made clear, and the two main characters' most essential traits are identified. And the history of their marriage—what compelled each one to marry the other—is emphasized.

These five introductory pages to the story itself do *not* represent authorial throat clearing, of Gilchrist avoiding plunging into the actual plot; for she will prove time and again her understanding of the need for a short story to take off within the first sentence or two. In this instance, a relatively long introduction works because the reader *lets* it work. These five pages limn the two majors characters to such resonant effect that no reader will get impatient. It works because Gilchrist does what she needs to do to make it work.

At the story's *actual* beginning, Letty and Tom have been married now for 14 years, "and the Wilson's luck held."[18] Tom "stayed busy gambling and hunting and fishing and being the life of the party at the endless rounds of dinners and cocktail parties and benefits and Mardi Gras functions that consume the lives of the Roman Catholic hierarchy that dominates the life of the city that care forgot."[19] Letty, in the meantime, "was preoccupied with the details of their domestic life and her work in the community."[20] In other words, she's been doing what the wife of a banker *should* be doing.

Why, given the rather large frame here—the whole substance of one couple's marriage—does this piece stand as a *real* short story? The short story, by tradition, focuses on an isolated moment that, because of its importance and resonance, serves to imply the whole essence of a situation or the major essence of a character. What saves this particular story from being merely an "outline" for a novel that for some reason Gilchrist never expanded, or from being a flabby, overly upholstered "short" story that actually contains too much material to stay buoyant? The answer is that through it all Gilchrist pursues one thread: Tom and Letty's "richness." In several ways were the Wilsons rich. They "grew rich in houses"[21]—in addition to their big house in the Garden District, they also have a weekend home on Lake Ponchartrain, a duck camp, and a French Quarter apartment. Tom was "rich in being satisfied to sleep with his wife,"[22] not a standard situation in their social setting, to be sure. And the Wilsons were rich "in common sense."[23] When it seemed Letty could not conceive, they adopted a baby girl and "everyone swore she even walked and talked like Tom."[24] (And in a relatively minor manifestation of their richness, but one that will play a poignant role in how the story ends, Tom begins raising good-quality Labrador retrievers.) After the Wilsons adopted the little girl they named Helen, they had a number of their own children, and they "became so rich in children the neighbors all lost count."[25] But Helen suffered from dyslexia, "a complicated learning disability that is a fashionable problem with children in New Orleans."[26]

(Helen's doctor is a very minor character, but Gilchrist's thumbnail description of him reveals her swift indelibility in painting a verbal picture; she sees him "crossing his short legs and settling his steel-rimmed glasses on his nose like a tiny bicycle stuck on a hill."[27])

Also, the Wilsons were "rich in maids,"[28] which was necessary, given the care needed by all those children.

The several ways in which the Wilsons are rich—Gilchrist's continued citing of the various aspects of their richness—is the tie that binds. The technique makes a long story tight. The tracking of this one particular thread ensures this is a real short story, keeps it an impressively effective short story; obviously, the opposite effect could have happened if more than one of the threads of the Wilsons' marriage were pursued.

The Wilsons' richness ends, however. The little adopted daughter, Helen, causes the maids much trouble; and one day she accidentally knocks over the bassinet with the new baby in it, and the baby is struck on the head and dies. "[N]o one came to the funeral but the family. Letty wore a plain dress she would wear any day."[29] The post-funeral reception "looked like the biggest cocktail party ever held in New Orleans. It took four rented butlers just to serve the drinks. Everyone wanted to get in on the Wilsons' tragedy."[30]

Tom begins to break down. Physical problems are accompanied by psychological ones. He loses his appeal. "Not as many people at the bank wanted to go out to lunch with him anymore. They were sick and tired of pretending his expensive mistakes were jokes."[31] And he is haunted by the tragic death of their baby, spending a lot of time thinking about Helen. "She looked so much like him that he believed people would think she was his illegitimate child. The more he tried to think himself into believing the baby's death was an accident, the more obstinate he became."[32] Contrary to how he and Letty have behaved with their children up to this point, when Tom catches Helen playing with one of his expensive Lab pups, he spanks her.

On top of all this, Letty fears she is pregnant again. As she lies abed, sick to her stomach, waiting to hear from the doctor to confirm her suspicions, Tom looks out the window and sees Helen once again playing with the puppy. Suddenly he decides to spend the night at his duck-hunting lodge. From the porch, he calls to Helen, telling her to come and get some play clothes and bring the dog; she is going with him to the duck camp. At this point, Gilchrist brings violence into the story, not an unusual maneuver for her. She views violence as a not uncommon aspect of contemporary life: violence between friends and neighbors, between family members or lovers, or randomly between complete strangers. Her fiction, as we will see as we proceed through our analysis book by book, documents instances of cruelty to the point of physical threat or even harm.

And that is certainly the case here. At the duck-hunting lodge, Tom takes a rifle and shoots the dog and shoots Helen; then he steps outside and puts a bullet through his own head. Gilchrist ends the story on a "social" note: the social reaction to what has taken place at the lodge. "No one, not even the district attorney of New Orleans, wanted to believe a man would shoot a $3,000 Labrador retriever sired by Super Chief out of Prestidigitation."[33]

This is a story that jolts and jars, but it is also a story that demonstrates Gilchrist's ability in the short story form and her respect for its difference from the novel. It is, however, missing (through no fault of its own or the fault of the author) *the* element by which Gilchrist has come to be best known and by which she had gathered her devoted readership: it does not feature one of her strongly drawn, convention-defying female characters. In "Rich," the husband, Tom, dominates the story, and Letty dwells in his shadow, exactly where such a tradition-adhering, even convention-worshipping, wife would live. But, on the other hand, we can let the absence of such a feature—such a character, that is—actually work for us, because Letty, in her consummate conventionality, sets up a good contrast to the strong female protagonists whom Gilchrist introduces in subsequent stories in this collection. Letty stands as the *not* praiseworthy opposite.

In fact, *In the Land of Dreamy Dreams* introduces two of Gilchrist's most famous female characters, who will make frequent appearances throughout her fiction. Rhoda Manning and Nora Jane Whittington are these two characters, both making debuts here; Rhoda appears in four of the stories and Nora Jane in one. This creative use of recurrent characters is the most readily obvious trait of Gilchrist's short stories and novels. Tracking these recurrent characters through her entire oeuvre, which I will do in the pages that follow, gives witness to the characters' evolution as personalities forged by having to undergo significant adjustments as the years—as their lives—advance. Gilchrist makes it possible to watch and follow these recurrent characters, and get to know them on a people-next-door basis of familiarity. Rhoda Manning is not identical to Nora Jane Whittington, and vice versa. Gilchrist has created them distinctive from one another, and from all other of her other recurrent characters that will make appearances in later short story collections and novels.

She addresses the practice of using recurrent characters in her journal, *Falling through Space*, in which she posits, in a general way, "there may be a limited number of characters any one writer can create and perhaps a limited number of stories any writer can tell." From there, she goes on to personalizes the issue: "It's gotten to the point where it's impossible for me to create new characters because the old ones keep grabbing up all the roles."[34]

Rhoda Manning makes her debut in the story "1957, A Romance." The title is ironic, as I will explain later; for it is hardly a romance in the sense of an unsubtle, sentimental love story. It is actually about love gone awry, soured. This story is placed in the second section of the collection, which is called "Things Like the Truth"; and all four of the stories in this section are dreary—this one in which Rhoda debuts being no exception. "1957, a Romance" ushers the reader directly into the action, with a short opening paragraph establishing the basics of the situation at hand. The time of year is June, the setting northern Alabama. "Upstairs Rhoda's small sons lay sleeping. Somewhere in North Carolina her young husband sulked because she'd left him."[35] (A reader new to Gilchrist, having picked up this collection to read first, and thus proceeding through the stories in the order in which they are presented, should be advised that although the character of Rhoda sees the first light of day in print not as a new-born but as a young woman, she will indeed be seen in childhood later in the collection; and that this collection, along with Gilchrist's later books, will come to offer in their cumulative effect a composite picture of Rhoda's life up to the point of her middle-middle-age.)

But in this grim story in which she makes her first entrance onto the stage, why she has left her husband and come back home to her parents is soon made obvious: she is seeking an abortion. An important aspect of Rhoda's life and character is aired in this first story about her, which is the continued importance of her father to her life. Arguably, it is *the* most important factor in Rhoda's life and how she grew up. As I will show, it is the greatest connective thread through all of the Rhoda stories. So, in this instance, in her abject desire *not* to have another baby, Rhoda turns to the person she always turns to in a crunch: "Daddy." To her father, she insists she can't undergo another cesarean and thus she needs to terminate her pregnancy.

From the local gynecologist she has obtained the name of a doctor who would do the procedure. This information is obtained from him by the way a woman can often get something she wants—by sex. But Rhoda also needs $500; and this is where Daddy comes in—but without Rhoda's mother's knowledge of the real reason for Rhoda's visit back home. To Daddy, Rhoda insists that getting pregnant again was not her fault, that her husband did it on purpose to keep her from leaving him. A quick insight into Rhoda's character is offered by Gilchrist in saying that Rhoda "always believed her own stories as soon as she told them."[36]

To himself, her father admits that he has spoiled her; to Rhoda he promises to take care of the problem. The name that Rhoda obtained from the gynecologist is a doctor in Houston, and her father accompanies her there, but first he fabricates a reason for the trip to Rhoda's mother. Here in our first encounter with Rhoda, who do we see her turning to solve the emotional and financial predicament she is in? Certainly not her mother, who is actually kept in the dark about what's really going on here, for fear—both Rhoda's fear and her father's fear—that Rhoda's mother would be unable to handle the situation, being the traditional "little woman" that she is. Rhoda turns to a man; and not simply any man, but Daddy.

But with this brushstroke that rounds out the mother's character to be more than just "a gentle, religious woman who lived her life in service to her family and friends," Gilchrist reveals "she had spells of fighting back against the terrible inroads they [family and friends] made into her small personal life."[37] Although unaware of Rhoda's plans for an abortion, her mother nevertheless puts forth one of her fighting-back spells now—over the issue of Rhoda leaving her husband (for the third time in two years). Rhoda, by her mother's estimation, "was the most demanding of her four children, the only daughter, the most unpredictable, the hardest to control or understand;"[38] and nothing, apparently, is about to change this outlook.

On the other hand, let us not be too harsh on Rhoda for her dependence on her father; it is 1957, after all. Her spunk and willfulness notwithstanding, she can not be separated from her time and still retain authenticity as a character. What is most telling at this point, in this debut-of-Rhoda story, is that out of her mother's traditionalism and the supposed need for her mother to be sheltered, we can observe in her reaction to her daughter traces of the very belligerence she finds so offensive in Rhoda. She is her mother's daughter. And this is an ironic yet interesting concept, since in this story and in the subsequent Rhoda stories as well as in the one Rhoda novel Gilchrist has written so far, *Net of Jewels*, Rhoda is as dismissive of her mother as she is obsessive about earning her father's love. This could be seen as a case of turning away from the parent you most resemble and toward the one you *want* to be like; of not wanting to recognize, as in Rhoda's case, that a large amount of her mother's dual footing in demure wifely posture and fight-back attitude—which results in feelings of awkwardness as well as ambivalence about self-assertiveness—is also found in herself. At the same time, Rhoda, as we will come to see as we analyze further Rhoda stories and the one Rhoda novel, will never stop struggling to free herself from her father's dominating influence. The other side of *that* coin is her father's dichotomous behavior toward her: indulgent one minute and critical the next minute. This shifting and apparently inconsistent attitude toward her parents adds up to a crucial factor in critically estimating Gilchrist's fiction: how life-like, realistic, authentic, and personal is her conception and presentation of the character of Rhoda Manning.

The plan, then, is for Daddy to drive Rhoda up to Nashville to catch a plane to Houston. On the way to Nashville, her father's impatience flares. Rhoda is reading Hemingway and expresses how wooed she is by his writing. Daddy insists "I don't know why you want to fill up your head with all that stuff. No wonder you don't have any sense, Rhoda." But her father is nothing if not capable of quick reversals in his attitude toward his daughter, and now tells himself "nothing will ever hurt her. As long as I live nothing will ever harm her."[39]

After the abortion procedure itself, once back in her room in the hotel they stayed in, "whenever she woke up [Daddy] was there beside her and nothing could harm her ever as long as he lived."[40] At one point in Rhoda's sleep, she dreams of "leaning across a table staring into Ernest Hemingway's eyes as he lit her cigarette."[41] Here is the element of romance suggested by the story's title, then; but this little romantic fantasy stands thinly next to the experience Rhoda has just undergone. But the title of the story is of course ironic.

On the way home from Houston to Alabama, Rhoda and her father stop in at the Fourth of July family reunion. When her uncle James, an eye surgeon, learns from her that no preliminary tests were done to establish the fact that she was indeed pregnant, he suggests that she was imagining herself to be so because she dreaded *being* pregnant so much. Rhoda dismisses his idea, insisting she didn't really care if she were pregnant or not. "'I'm beautiful,' she thought, running her hands over her body. 'I'm skinny and I'm beautiful and no one is ever going to cut me open. I'm skinny and beautiful and no one can make me do anything.'"[42]

At this first encounter with Rhoda Manning, she is age 19, an independent spirit only up to a point, for she remains reliant on men to a large degree and selfish to an even greater degree. Despite the gray tone of the story, its less than buoyant mood, Rhoda holds the reader's attention and interest; and in three other stories in this collection, Rhoda, as a child in these instances, holds reader interest even more closely.

"Revenge" is a well-executed story; it is tight in scope and in the "single-effect" quality that traditionally defines the short story form. And the two stories that are companions to it, "1944" and "Perils of the Nile," share with it this clean, lean, slice-of-life and single-facet-of-a-character capacity that the short story can achieve and at which Gilchrist is so adept.

"Revenge" opens with a compelling, inviting first line: "It was the summer of the Broad Jump Pit."[43] The setting is Mississippi during World War II. Ten-year-old Rhoda, who narrates the story, is "the only girl in a house full of cousins." There are six of these cousins, "shipped to the Delta for the summer, dumped on my grandmother."[44] Her father is doing war work, and she and her siblings and mother are living in Indiana for the duration of the conflict.

The broad jump pit is dug in the middle of a pasture that summer on behest of Rhoda's father, who admonishes Rhoda's 13-year-old brother Dudley and the other boy cousins by way of V-Mail letter to begin training for the Olympic Games that are sure to be resumed once the Allies win. The letter also instructed Dudley to take good care of Rhoda, their "father's own dear sweet little girl."[45]

Rhoda doesn't want to be treated as a dear sweet little girl but, instead, wants to be in on the thrilling action happening around the broad jump pit. The focus of her angst is her brother Dudley, who dismisses Rhoda's interest and presence; he insists that this is serious business suitable only for boys.

Predictably, Dudley's attitude does not sit well with Rhoda. Her grandmother adds fuel to the fire by planning for Rhoda to go over to a neighboring plantation to play with a little girl there. Rhoda's temper flares and she begins calling people the most outrageous thing she can say in the South during the war: "goddamned nigger German spy."[46]

All Rhoda has left to do, then, is observe the boys' training from a distance. The divide between her and the boys widens. She spies on them constantly, from every different angle, yelling insults; but the boys, led by her brother, ignore her. Rhoda's reaction to the continued exclusion is this: "I began to pray the Japs would win the war, would come marching into Issaquena Country and take them prisoners, starving them and torturing them, sticking bamboo splinters under their fingernails. I saw myself in the Japanese colonel's office, turning them in, writing their names down, myself being treated like an honored guest, drinking tea from tiny blue cups like the ones the Chinaman had in his store."[47]

Rhoda is only ten years old, but she obviously is aware of current events, apparently listening to radio news or to adults over the back fence. She also exhibits how "topical" she is in her knowledge of the outside world when she then wishes the boys would get polio and have to live in iron lungs. She is not cruel. She is simply a child, and one whose childishness is heightened by being left out of other children's games, particularly a game that is such serious business. Gilchrist is accurately writing from the point of view of a precocious child conjuring the current-to-the-times "bogeyman." Meanwhile, Rhoda focuses on the "girl" stuff available to her—namely, practicing her dancing with her grandmother's housekeeper. While Rhoda and Baby Doll dance inside, the Mississippi summer holds full sway out of doors; and Gilchrist eloquently describes it: "Outside the summer sun beat down on the Delta, beating down a million volts a minute, feeding the soybeans and cotton and clover, sucking Steele's Bayou up into the clouds, beating down on the road and the store, on the pecans and elms and magnolias, on the men at work in the fields, on the athletes at work in the pasture."[48]

But the broad jump pit haunts her, and she and her brother grow increasingly fractious, until one day something comes along to take Rhoda's mind off it: the announcement by Rhoda's cousin Lauralee that she is to be married in a week's time. Rhoda is in awe of her grown-up cousin, who is nothing less than splendid. Lauralee asks Rhoda to perform a very adult job: be her maid of honor. Rhoda gets to pick out a new dress: a "girl" treat. Rhoda is experiencing her own kind of success without the participation of or even cooperation from the boys. Is Rhoda a budding feminist when she insists to her cousin she herself is never getting married but, instead, plans to go to New York to be a lawyer? Has being kept out of the boys' games ironically hardened her against traditional females roles and made her decide she will do adult boys' things like move away and never have children and be a lawyer? No, it simply means that Gilchrist is accurate in her take on how a little girl at this time in her life and at this place and time in history sees things.

Rhoda selects a dress, finds that she adores the groom when he arrives, but is disappointed in the wedding itself. She finds the reception more agreeable, receiving compliments on her dress, eating cake, and letting people hug her. Then she goes to make herself a drink! Her feelings are quite buoyant. Outside, "a full moon was caught like a kite in the pecan trees across the river."[49]

But then Rhoda succumbs to acting rashly; she leaves the porch at night, something she's never done before. There in the near distance is the broad jump pit, "unguarded." She runs down there, discards her new dress (shedding the *girl stuff*), and with pole in hand and subsequently into the cup, sails over the barrier. The story ends: "Sometimes I think whatever has happened since has been of no real interest to me"[50]—putting a positive, upbeat, and resonant final spin on a humorous and psychologically strong story.

"1944" is a brief piece, again told with psychological accuracy from a child's point of view; in this story Rhoda is eight years old and living up north with her family for the duration of the war. Rhoda scorns her piano teacher, feeling that she is an "old German spy"[51] and jealous of Rhoda's talent. (Already Rhoda demonstrates how full she is of herself—a trait that will not diminish as Rhoda grows over the course of the many stories Gilchrist writes about her.) But one night she meets "a glamorous war widow"[52] and she and Rhoda make delightful music tapping nine martini glasses, Rhoda realizing from the experience that cooperative effort is the true way of producing good music. The reader assumes or at least hopes Rhoda will extrapolate this lesson into a lesson in life in general: that to be headstrong and independent is not always the right course.

"Perils of the Nile" finds Rhoda in the sixth grade. At the story's opening, she is arising from her seat at the Saturday movie matinee and looking around for any boys she likes; she sees only Bebber Dyson, who is of little interest to her because of his dark looks and small stature—and because he is poor (although he had given her an early instruction in sex when he showed her a book of dirty cartoons). He is her school's best basketball player, a "mystery" to her that he should be so good at it, since he didn't have a good home life, his father was a drunk, and he lived in a house that wasn't a house at all but just rooms rented above a store. To be good at basketball, according to Rhoda's thinking, a person has to have the right equipment as well as a good diet and understanding parents. But then Rhoda decides perhaps the truth is that "you have to be poor to be a good basketball player."[53] But that line of thinking leads Rhoda to another contradiction presented by Bebber: that he hadn't the smell usual to poor people.

Bebber falls in along side Rhoda as they proceed up the aisle of the movie theater. He asks if she would like to go with him to hang out at the drugstore. She agrees to it, not certain his company is such a good idea in the interests of social prestige, but at least she was going to the drugstore with a boy. She shows off something new to him: holding out her hand, where, on one of her fingers, a pearl ring is supposed to be; but she discovers it's gone, the heirloom she had received in the mail for graduation that very morning. Bebber helps her look for it.

This story suffers from a technical problem that will recur in Gilchrist's short stories, which is her abrupt, whiplash shifts in point-of-view. Generally speaking, short stories have little room to accommodate point-of-view shifts. Successful exceptions to that rule are possible, and Gilchrist herself will, even in later stories in this first collection, proffer workable exceptions; an exception to the rule has to do with the lack of *abruptness* in the shift from one point of view to another. The raison d'etre of a short story is its leanness—"meanness," in a way of looking at it—in depicting one aspect of a character or one situation that displays the character in a most telling light. Quick, sudden changes in point of view muddy the effect of what a short story can accomplish; it breaks, too suddenly, the reader's focus on the character standing right in front of them at the moment. By common wisdom a short story has only the resources to focus on one character. To achieve its most effectiveness, a short story concentrates a spotlight on one character performing in one event, or in only a limited few events, that transpire in a relatively short span of time but which go a long way toward revealing the character's essential nature. Or, as we saw in Gilchrist's story "Rich," it can also arrive at an effectiveness by following one certain strain in a character's life—such as Tom's richness in all things—through a long period of time to see how this one particular factor, and, really, only this *one* certain factor, plays out in

dictating the whole contour of the person's life: in Tom's case, ironically leading to his suicide.

But in a story such as "Perils of the Nile," in which the author lets one
event speak for a universe of events that virtually, in their implied and suggested totality, amount to the whole character and his or her life, to suddenly—emphasis here on *suddenly*—introduce another character's
perspective on that event does not come across as the author casting valuable
light on the situation but as an inadvertent and detrimental sidetracking of
the reader's concentration, a distraction from finding out the essential information about the story's primary character. And, further, a short story is, not
only by general rule but also by practical necessity dictated by its limited
space, all about *one* character. Here in this particular story about Rhoda, this
is how the problem of abrupt point of view shifts manifests itself: while
Rhoda and her friend Bebber search on the floor of the movie theater for her
antique pearl ring we suddenly get Bebber's reactions to Rhoda, including
such impressions as the "sweet sweaty smell of her blouse," that she is a
"strange girl," and that she has a beautiful mother.[54]

Does the interruption contribute to a developing picture of Rhoda? No,
what information it *does* supply toward that end is not worth the head-jerking
distraction *away* from Rhoda. It interferes with the reader's concentration; it
is like someone talking in your ear, making brief asides, while you are at the
same time involved in a conversation with another person. You don't really
register what this person who is half-whispering in your ear is saying, only
that the voice is irritating.

Rhoda and Bebber continue to look for the ring, and another jarring
intrusion of Bebber's point of view occurs. He finds the ring on the floor and
pockets it without mentioning the discovery to Rhoda. This is an important
event in the development of the story, to be sure, but now—to continue the
metaphor of the previous paragraph—because this irritating voice persists in
buzzing in your ear, the need to reduce two concurrent stimuli down to one
can actually lead to turning away from the person with who you are actually
involved in a conversation to listen to the person whispering in your ear—in
this case, going off track and wondering about Bebber too much. What are
the real situations behind the rather pathetic view Rhoda holds of him? The
road has divided, but a successful short story cannot afford a fork in the road,
even if the reader is soon yanked back from the dead-end fork and plopped
back onto the main line: in this instance, of course, the main line being
Rhoda and her story, not Bebber and his story. The reader's concentration

has been broken, and the fracture does not mend; readers arrive at the end of the story with more things on their minds than necessary—or more than is safe for the ultimate good of the story.

Thinking the ring lost forever, Rhoda goes home, feeling very sorry for herself: "Every time something happens it happens to me."[55] (This self-centered attitude Rhoda will possess throughout her life, throughout all the Rhoda stories to come.) It occurs to her that she might pray for the ring's return, but Rhoda and religion are not on the best of terms; however, losing the ring indeed represents a crisis in her life. She attempts a bargain, promising Jesus to go to Sunday school every Sunday if she can find her ring.

Gilchrist ends the story in the wrong place: with Bebber going home, taking the ring out of his pocket, and thinking about Rhoda's mother. "The ring . . . like her, elegant and still and foreign [being from the South, that is]." He cleans himself to a spic-and-span shine and proceeds to take the ring to Rhoda—but, actually, just taking it to her because that is where her mother is—"the rays of the setting sun making a path all the way to her house, a little road to travel, a wide band of luminous and precarious order."[56]

This is a beautifully written passage, but it is not about Rhoda. Ending the story from Bebber's point of view leaves the reader perplexed that this has become Bebber's story instead of Rhoda's; for the ending is about Bebber's callow romanticism, and what does that contribute to the story's initial intent, which was to show an aspect of Rhoda's childhood manipulation of the male of the species? The way Gilchrist ends the story, then, it is not so much a wrapping up of this event in Rhoda's young life as it is a frustrating invitation for the reader to once again want to know more about Bebber.

The story "The Famous Poll at Jody's Bar," however, not only introduces another one of Gilchrist's best drawn and most frequently recurring characters, Nora Jane Whittington, but also demonstrates how Gilchrist ironically can make her tendency toward shifting points of view an *effective* technique. In fact, "Famous Poll" is not only one the best stories in the *Dreamy Dreams* collection but also one of the best stories Gilchrist has ever written. Her ability with swift, concrete scene setting is in full display, ushering the reader quickly into the plot and, at the same time, by the following passage, imparting a fast yet indelible first impression of her main character, Nora: "It was ninety-eight degrees in the shade in New Orleans, a record-breaking day in August. Nora Jane Whittington sat in a small apartment several blocks from Jody's Bar and went over her alternatives. 'No two ways about it,' she said to herself, shaking out her black curls, 'if Sandy want my ass in San Jose, I'm taking it to San Jose. But I've got to get some cash.' Nora Jane was nineteen years old, a self-taught anarchist and a quick-change artist."[57]

Gilchrist goes on to elaborate on Nora Jane's ability to disguise herself. "She could turn her graceful body into any character she saw in a movie or on T.V. Her specialties were boyish young lesbians, boyish young nuns, and a variety of lady tourists."[58] But Nora Jane has no happy home life; it is learned immediately that her father died in the early years of the Vietnam War and that her mother is an alcoholic, and the sisters of the Academy of the Most Holy Name of Jesus, which Nora Jane attends, plead with Nora Jane's mother to forsake her drinking or put Nora Jane in a Catholic boarding school.

Nora Jane, being a true Gilchrist female protagonist, has her own ideas about what is really important in her life: not a decent home, but a boyfriend. Then right after graduating from high school, she met Sandy. Sandy is concisely spelled out by way of Gilchrist's dexterous, brief, but distinct verbal picture-making: "He was fresh out of a Texas reform school with $500.00 in the bank and a new lease on life. He was a handsome boy with green eyes as opaque and unfathomable as a salt lake."[59]

With no excessive detail—with every detail that *is* given contributing to the story's effectiveness—Nora Jane's and Sandy's brief courtship is traced, from the point of their first "date"—attending a political rally in Audubon Park—to, at the end of that day, Sandy asking Nora Jane if she would like to stay at his place for a while; and it turned out she stayed for 14 months.

Sandy teaches Nora Jane what he knows best: how to make a living stealing. And when knocking off a certain beauty parlor proves quite lucrative, Sandy takes off, heading for the West Coast, leaving Nora Jane behind with the promise that he will send for her when he got settled.

So, Nora Jane, having been tutored well, has come up with a plan for joining Sandy in California: robbing a neighborhood bar there in New Orleans. She is young and naïve but determined. Although she has never "been out of the state of Louisiana, but once settled on a plan of action she was certain all she needed was a little luck and she was as good as wading in the Pacific Ocean. One evening's work and her hands were back in Sandy's hair."[60]

At this point in the story, Gilchrist changes the point of view—again, in mid-stream. In this case, though, it does no damage to the story's effectiveness; in fact, it makes sense to do it. This new portion of the story *not* being told from Nora Jane's point of view is set off with roman numerals: "II," as if it were a separate chapter. The point of view in this three-and-a-half-page section is omniscient; the reader is ushered into Jody's Bar, the joint Nora Jane is playing to knock over, and given a look around. There is nothing jarring about this procedure; the story isn't sent off balance by this separate, omniscient section, the purpose of which is to limn the atmosphere of the place into which Nora Jane will be stepping. A richer story results when readers are let in on what was transpiring in the establishment before the advent of the gun-toting Nora Jane, with robbery in mind.

What is going on at Jody's on this hot Saturday morning is the poll. Wesley Labouisse is conducting a poll to see if people think Prescott Hamilton IV should really be marrying Emily Anne Hughes. The story then shifts back to Nora Jane, and it certainly is not a bothersome shift; the reader is ready for it, having now gathered an informative picture of the patrons, employees, and today activities in Jody's Bar. Nora Jane has prepared for her deed by dumping most of her possessions in a box for charity and burning Sandy's letters (so he wouldn't be implicated in her crime if she were caught); and she leaves her place carrying a leather bag in which she has placed her costume change and her bus ticket to San Francisco. And a gun, too.

Meanwhile the poll continues at the bar. Nora Jane enters. Now the two halves of the story are brought together, two streams flowing together to make a mightier one. Nora Jane demonstrates both spunk and cleverness in handling the actual robbery. She insists that everyone in the joint put their hands over their heads, locks the door, pulls down the "Closed" sign, and makes them all go into the ladies' room, informing her hostages that their speed in cooperation is necessary to avoid the result of her anger; she adds that, with her being a run-away from a mental hospital, going unmedicated, anger is only a short reach away.

After locking the men in the ladies' room, Nora Jane changes into the costume she brought with her for her escape: a nun's habit; and she removes the cash from the register. As she leaves the bar, "as she passed the card table she stopped, marked a ballot, folded it neatly, and dropped it into the Mason jar."[61]

With money in hand, she now can go west to be with Sandy; and with determination, with her true grit, she "mak[es] her a path all the way to mountains and valleys and fields, to rivers and streams and oceans. To a boy who was like no other. To the source of all water."[62] Nora Jane weaves her independence with the threads of headstrongness, intrepidness, freedom from self-doubt, and, although not so obvious in this first story in which she features, but as will be readily observable in subsequent Nora Jane stories, a strong sense of self-preservation.

In the three stories so far in which Rhoda Manning has figured as a young girl, she is seen as selfish in her pursuit of self-expression; and in the one story in which she is a young wife and mother, again, she is selfish, and her needs are paramount over other people's.

In Nora Jane stories to come, Nora Jane's self-preservation will extend to the new family she creates in California, and she will establish herself very quickly in the reader's eyes as the most admirable of Gilchrist's recurrent characters. In further Rhoda stories, Rhoda will finally—but it will take a long while—soften in her self-centeredness; and her path to that end is no less interesting to follow than Nora Jane's path to a successful family life out West.

Other excellent stories in this collection include, for instance, the title story, which offers a funny, sly examination of New Orleans high society by spotlighting the local country club, where the old guard—upper-middle-class southern whites—is threatened by intruders from outside their hermetically sealed world. This comfortable New Orleans society is again given a pinch and a poke in "The President of the Louisiana Live Oak Society," in which a baby-blue-Lincoln-Continental–driving mother can not keep her teenage son out of the drug world. The main character in "Summer, an Elegy" is eight-year-old Shelby; the time is the years of World War II, the place the Mississippi Delta. Shelby has quite an imagination, and is given to truth stretching; and this particular summer is the summer of his growing sexual awareness and experimentation.

But there are a few less-than-successful pieces to be found here, too. A prime example of the stories that do not need to be read a second time is "Suicides." This is a grim, underdeveloped narrative about the fragility of the human psyche. Gilchrist's ability with the "quick picture" works against her here, for this story begs more questions than it answers, and its point remains too elusive—not in a provocatively vague way, which short stories *can* be good at, but in a way that compels the puzzled reader to wonder what her purpose was here.

Despite some weaknesses, *In the Land of Dreamy Dreams* is a powerful collection overall, and one that introduces readers to this unique Southern voice.

Chapter 3

Gilchrist's First Novel
(*The Annunciation*)

THE ANNUNCIATION SCENE FROM THE BIBLE presented one of the most widely used and inherently beautiful motifs in Renaissance art. An epitome of the depiction of that motif is Fra Angelico's *Annunciation* fresco at the Convent of San Marco in Florence, Italy. The scene captured there, as well as in all other Annunciation scenes, is, of course, the archangel Gabriel's advent on bended knee to announce to Mary that she is to be delivered of the Son of God. Annunciation scenes—*l'Annunciaziona*, in the original Italian—brim with Christian symbolism, and, despite variations in detail, all share one common aspect: the archangel Gabriel acting in honor and supplication, like a suitor pressing his suit, and Mary hearing his stirring news with modesty, acquiescence, and fortitude.

Ellen Gilchrist's first novel, published in 1983, is appropriately titled *The Annunciation*, because it contains an Annunciation scene—actually, it presents more than one instance of the announcing and receiving of news. And on an even broader, more general level, the novel as a *whole* is an annunciation: the announcing of a new life for the primary character. Like Gilchrist's first collection of short stories, *The Annunciation* remains in print, a testament to its quality. But is it perfect? Indeed not. Did it set a high-water mark for subsequent novels as *In the Land of Dreamy Dreams* did for her further story collections? Not quite. In terms of sheer artistry, it does not stand eye-to-eye with *Dreamy Dreams*; and comparing her first collection of short stories and her first novel so early in her career suggests that her greater strength lay in the short story form rather than in the novel—but such a conclusion is really too premature to draw so early in this study. It is more appropriate at this point to see her first novel simply as that; and *The Annunciation* is a strong first novel. Its warmth and humanity are impressive.

Basically the novel is about a woman's gaining in confidence, her learning to make positive choices, and her eschewing of victimhood. It is about a woman's learning not to suffer from her choices based on lack of experience or on comfort and safety, which result in her taking herself to wrong places that represent settling rather than growth—settling, that is, for the closest, easiest shelter in life. Further, the novel is about a woman exploring what it means to be her own person to the point where, at the novel's end, she has so advanced herself that she can say, "My will be done."

The novel begins in familiar Gilchrist territory: the Mississippi Delta— specifically on Esperanza Plantation, where Amanda McCamey, when we first encounter her, is only four years old, fatherless, but already having fallen completely under the thrall of her first cousin, Guy, who will continue to exert a considerable and disturbing influence on her life long after she has moved away from the Delta. "Amanda thinks Guy hung the moon, they said. She thinks Guy can do no wrong. She likes Guy the best of everyone in the whole delta."[1] Something very serious grows between Amanda and Guy during the childhood they spend at the Plantation. "Everyone on Esperanza watched it, but only the black people knew what they were watching. Only the black people knew what it meant."[2]

What *it* meant was love beyond the bounds of traditional cousin-love, because, on the eve of Guy's departure for college, they have sex, and Amanda gets pregnant. She is only 15, but she nevertheless undergoes a cesarean, and her baby girl is taken from her to be put up for adoption. Amanda's grandmother sends her off to school in Virginia where "you can be a girl again."[3]

The novel's title *The Annunciation* would imply the impending arrival of a very special child. Although there is no scene here—elaborately done or not—in which Amanda's pregnancy is announced and explained to her, and although she spends the months of her pregnancy in a home for unwed mothers in New Orleans, hardly the milieu in which we might expect an exceptional baby to be gestating; despite all this, the baby is very special indeed, at least in terms of the story told here—Amanda's life story, that is. Although taken from Amanda, her child's absence will haunt her every day of her life.

Despite family law dictating that Amanda and her cousin Guy are not supposed to be in touch, they defy that ruling and *do* stay in touch; in fact, in the spring of her first year at the Virginia Seminary, Guy comes to visit her. He is a football hero at Ole Miss, and Amanda has lost none of her infatuation with him. She is still dependent on him and self-abnegating before him. Waiting for his visit, she was "hardly daring to believe he was really on his way to see her, driving all that way to be with her for a few hours. It seemed more like something she would do than something he would do."[4]

To use contemporary phraseology, the relationship is "unhealthy," which of course is not simply a reference to their genetic closeness. The relationship's unhealthiness really arises from its self-destructiveness for Amanda. To be a fully realized person, an individual, to have one's own integrity, sensibilities, and opinions and ideas, for Amanda to have personal parameters defining her as a being separate from all other beings—for all this to happen, she can not continue this relationship with her cousin. In his presence, she has no cell walls; molecularly, she is fused with him when in his company. This is the "battle" of the novel, the central conflict that is the axis upon which all the plot revolves: Amanda's finding an identity *separate* from Guy's.

And certainly the battle is far from won at the time of Guy's visit to her at her Virginia school. Amanda shouts at him to make love to her. Guy refuses actual intercourse but introduces her to a whole new program of sexual activities just short of that. Guy has sworn to God he would never have intercourse with her again, a position and a promise *not* indicating he has decided to take a high moral road: the other things he does to her and has her do to him suggest otherwise. No, his oath before God has as its provenance his fear of getting caught at it by her getting pregnant again.

Guy is less and less a likable character as the novel progresses, and readers can not help but applaud Amanda as *she* makes progress—slow progress, to be sure—in removing herself from her cousin's domination. But it takes a long time.

Amanda has told herself since the birth of her baby that no one will ever make her do what she doesn't want to do. (Echoes of Scarlett O'Hara swearing she will never go hungry again.) The main point of this mantra that she repeats to herself is, of course, that no one can keep her from seeing Guy.

Amanda is self-consumed; she is full of herself. She is, so far, hardly easier for the reader to care about than Guy. After all, selfishness and self-destructiveness are what define her up to this point. Her love for Guy shows no strength of character, only the opposite, for it is "easy" love. It is an ironically "safe" one, despite the legal and social strictures against first-cousin relationships. It is safe because it is the most available one to her; Guy is the most available male figure, in the absence of her father—who, we have previously learned, died when Amanda was very young—to give warmth and comfort to the side of Amanda that is still a little girl, and to provide the sexual attention that the burgeoning woman side of her is beginning to crave. So what if an unwanted pregnancy is the result? The safe harbor of Guy is worth the risk.

While at school, Amanda suffers abdominal pain, which leads her to a clandestine doctor's appointment; the reader is informed, behind Amanda's back, as it were, that chances are not good that she will ever conceive again.

And that is exactly what happens when Amanda marries, and she and her husband attempt to have a baby. Malcolm Ashe, as Amanda describes him, is "this rich New Orleans Jew."[5] When Guy meets him several years after Amanda marries him, he finds Malcolm "handsome, well-mannered."[6] For his part, Malcolm is fascinated by Amanda's Delta plantation heritage, admitting to himself that "this is why he married Amanda, to be part of this world he liked to read about in books. He had been a Faulkner scholar at Yale, and it had a big effect on his life."[7]

So, anyway, years have passed, during which time Amanda has not seen Guy. He has moved to Chicago to play professional football. There he married a "sweet Italian girl"[9] whose rich father basically supports them, leaving Guy with lots of time on his hands. Meanwhile, Amanda is finding she hates New Orleans, "that old whore of a city."[9] Marriage to Malcolm enables her to travel in high society, but what is important to her is her work as a translator. (In her school days—back in the novel's earlier pages—we discovered that she excelled at learning languages, and now we learn that she took foreign-language classes at Tulane, where she soon became the "golden girl" for her felicitous translations of poetry.) This, then, is what she sees as her ticket out of her marriage and out of New Orleans, two sets of circumstances stultifying to her.

When Amanda's and Guy's grandmother dies out on the old Delta plantation, Guy comes home from Chicago, making this the first time he and Amanda have seen each other in a long time. "The old desire rose between them and they gave into it while outside the rain pounded down upon the houses on the streets and the leaves, upon the sidewalks and sheds and graves and clotheslines and fences. The old rain falling and falling all over the little town of Glen Allen, Mississippi."[10]

Why Amanda has such an aversion to her marriage and New Orleans is never made clear. This problem stems from the show-versus-tell issue in fictional technique. Amanda says she wants out of both, but Gilchrist simply hands the reader this information, as if insisting it be taken at face value, with few reasons and little proof offered. This situation amounts to a major flaw in the novel, for Amanda's attitude about her husband and the city they live in should be understood thoroughly before the reader can proceed to accept her negative attitude as the basis for what happens next.

Upon their encounter out on the plantation, on the occasion of their grandmother's death, Guy brings up to Amanda the delicate issue of the whereabouts of their daughter, who was given up for adoption many years ago. Guy wants to find her. Amanda has a sense that she is in New Orleans, adding to the complexity of the situation; but, on another front, she announces to Guy that she is intending to divorce Malcolm. Guy indicates he will leave his wife, insisting to Amanda that the two of them could build a life together.

Amanda refuses. "I want to find out what I really want in the world," she informs him. Now the true Amanda, an integrated and integral personality, can begin to emerge from the indistinct cloud of overdependence and finally gain shape and dimension in her own right.

Meanwhile Guy has had his and Amanda's daughter traced, and, finding out who she is, goes down to New Orleans—without Amanda's knowledge—and actually watches his now grown daughter at a tennis match. Meanwhile, too, Amanda has gotten comfortable with the arts crowd in New Orleans, one of whom is to be the catalyst for a remarkable turnabout in Amanda's life: the great crossroads that Amanda has been awaiting all her adult life, which will deepen the novel itself into something more profound than it has shown itself to be up to this point. This person—the catalyst—is potter Katie Dunbar, and she works at Tulane on a grant.

Not until this juncture in the novel—about a third of the way through—is the reader truly allowed under the skin of the novel. Until now, Gilchrist seemed to keep us outside the story, making us observe it from a distance, not quite letting us inside the characters to feel what they feel. But now, on the eve of Amanda's brand new life, Gilchrist finally burrows into Amanda's character and takes us with her, letting us see her from the inside out. Was this initial hesitation a failure of heart, or of technique, or of both? Is the novel's thinness up to this point, this sense on the reader's part of being rushed through it, there because Gilchrist's heart isn't in this part of the story—that Amanda hasn't really engaged *her* yet, either? If that was the case, should Gilchrist have dealt with these earlier episodes as flashbacks, with the actual focus of the novel trained on Amanda's life after leaving her marriage and New Orleans—both of which she will soon do? At any rate, the novel is now saved, which is the important thing.

Amanda and the potter Katie Dunbar quickly become close friends during the year the latter spends at Tulane. When Katie returns to her hometown of Fayetteville, Arkansas, Amanda is bereft. She goes to visit Katie and feels very comfortable in that university town in the Ozarks (where, of course, Gilchrist herself resides), gathering the sensation "It looks like where I am supposed to be."[12]

Correlative to Amanda doing the same thing, this is where the novel really comes alive.

Amanda returns to New Orleans, and "that fall a coincidence occurred."[13] It's almost too much of a coincidence for the narrative to bear, bordering on a "hand-of-God" intrusion into the plot exposition. But the truth is that the rest of the story could not happen without the coincidence's first taking place. The coincidence is this: Amanda is nearly finished with her graduate work in foreign languages at Tulane. One day she attends a translation seminar (the day she heard about the upcoming seminar, she unknowingly encountered her daughter, also a Tulane student—perhaps a laying on of the coincidence too thickly). The seminar is held by an eccentric scholar, who informs his audience of a manuscript of French poetry he recently smuggled out of the Vatican. He needs a good translator, and Amanda puts in a bid for the assignment. This cape-wearing old don lives in no other place than Fayetteville, Arkansas, where Amanda's new friend Katie lives.

Amanda insists to him, "I'll come up there and live and work with you."

Now her life is to change irrevocably. She asks Malcolm for a divorce before she goes; and before she goes, too, Gilchrist takes some time to acquaint readers with Amanda's daughter, a young New Orleans society matron, full of herself and of disdain for her life. To her therapist she insists, "You can't imagine what it's like to be locked up in this marriage,"[14] adding evidence to the old maxim that apples do indeed *not* fall too far from the tree.

But, right at this point, the novel is locked up, too, in an almost strangulating circle of coincidences, and the circle will have to be broken soon, or the novel will collapse under the weight of incredibility.

Off to Fayetteville Amanda goes. As her friend Katie the potter says, "There's always room for one more eccentric in the Ozarks."[15] Amanda secures a house for herself "built into the side of a small mountain."[16] Gilchrist's description of the town and its environs broadcasts her obvious love for it; and, incidentally, her words perform the same function as travel literature, making one long to see the place for oneself. Amanda encounters and embraces her life's fulfillment in this little university town, translating the old poetry of a French woman whom Amanda is not only beginning to get to know as an individual, but also with whom she is establishing a cross-centuries identity. "This is it, she thought. This is what I dreamed of. . . . Nothing scares me. . . ."[17] So this is Bohemia, she thought. I finally made it to the free people."[18] From this point in the novel till the end, Gilchrist allows the reader to experience Amanda becoming the person she truly is, as opposed to (as was the situation in the first third of the novel) the reader's simply being *told* things such as, most significantly, Amanda's discomfort with her life and marriage back in New Orleans.

Amanda's journey of self-discovery has a second catalyst. The first, of course, was Katie Dunbar the potter, whose friendship prompted Amanda's relocation to Fayetteville and her taking on the translation of French poems. Now her new self-realization comes to enjoy a big, breathing, living, corporeal symbol: Will Lyons, a good-looking mountain boy, in and out of college, working during the day and playing music in his free time. Amanda is by now in her early forties; Will is considerably younger. She and Will fall into a tumultuous affair, but at the same time they are both very shy of giving each other much indication of commitment, and tentative about admitting to love and the possibility of being loved by each other.

Just as Amanda is staking out her independence, a claim on it has arisen, and this is the big issue she is now faced with resolving. She must decide if independence, by definition, is *not* inclusive of a long, time-consuming relationship. When her baby was taken from her when she was still young, she swore she would never again let other people tell her what to do. This "doctrine" she had not completely followed until she left her marriage in New Orleans and began to establish herself in Fayetteville. Is letting Will into her life on a full-time basis a compromise of her doctrine of independence?

The rest of the novel, then, is delivered over to Amanda's attempt to come to a resolution. Every idea she has and mulls over about independence versus loving a man contributes to her believability as a character. The difficulty Amanda faces in balancing home life and career is ironically not helped by her good buddy Katie, herself quite an independent woman, who insists to Amanda that "If you can work and be in love at the same time, you're the first woman I ever knew that could."[19]

Amanda certainly does not believe her path will be smooth or well lighted, but she is determined to forge the path she feels necessary and most desirable for her. "I'm going to have my work and Will too," she insists.[20] But what adds a complication to Amanda's chosen path is that, at the same time, she is trying to maintain her independence in the face of her heart-stopping love for a man, he, Will, the young man she loves, is doing his own weighing of this relationship to determine his standing in it—specifically, *his* freedom to spend his own time in the fashion of his choosing. After all, Amanda is much older than he, she has a career, and she has money, all of which, in his estimation, adds up to power over him.

His desire to stand somewhat eye-to-eye financially with Amanda compels Will to take a good job offered to him on an oil rig in the Gulf, which necessitates a lengthy separation between them and a cutoff of communication. In his absence, arguably the most crucial event in Amanda's life occurs, or at least the single most important *positive* event in her *new* life occurs: she has a baby. It is Will's, of course; thus Amanda can indeed still conceive, despite what the doctor who had examined her back in her school days had believed after the birth of her first baby. The fact of her pregnancy comes to her in *the* Annunciation scene in the novel; and Gilchrist renders it without sentimentality. The role of the Archangel Gabriel is assumed by Luke, a medical school dropout, "the unwashed hippie doctor of the hills with his gorgeous tan." Luke bases his "diagnosis" on "a little configuration that appears in the eye" of pregnant women.[21]

The scene is moving, but not melodramatic. But to further complicate matters for Amanda, soon after she discovers her pregnancy, Guy comes from Chicago to visit her. Guy had been attempting to communicate with her ever since her relocation to Fayetteville, and now she sees him face to face for the first time since the death of their grandmother. In her vulnerable state—pregnant and with the father of her child incommunicado—Amanda, reverting not so much to old habits as that her old personality rears its head, clings to Guy upon his arrival and in tears. "Please take care of me," she says to him. "I'm tired of taking care of myself."[22] The reader can only shudder, wondering whether her newly found independence is collapsing. Amanda finds herself at a fragile point, and her return to Guy's shoulder to cry on *can* be understood. It is best understood as the need to find a familiar port in a storm, which is *not* a statement about the plot's predictability, because faith that this lapse is only temporary is never out of the reader's mind.

Guy once again presses Amanda to join him in confronting the woman in New Orleans who is their daughter and identifying themselves to her. Fortunately, this causes Amanda's "fever" to break, as it were. She recognizes anew that Guy is her past, that the daughter unknown to her is also her past. When faced with delving into her past, Amanda puts a hand up and says, "I'm going to stay right here on this mountain with this life I made for myself and finish finding out who I am. . . . I used to believe that the past was the present, that we could never leave it behind. Bullshit. The past is the past. You can dwell on it or you can move forward."[23]

Amanda does entertain the idea of abortion—even coming to the point of taking her friend Katie to a clinic with her—but ultimately she chooses to keep *this* baby. This baby *is* her new life. The letter she writes to Will *announcing* her pregnancy finally reaches him out on his oil rig; but she finds herself still haunted by the daughter she's never known. She wants to ask her daughter's forgiveness for abandoning her—again, an understandable sentiment, and this need to assuage her guilt does not represent a retraction on Amanda's part of her declaration of independence from her past.

On Christmas Eve, Will borrows a car and drives to Arkansas, but he stops in New Orleans on the way, having decided he will do this for Amanda: he will tell her daughter who her mother is. "This is what I'm supposed to do,"[24] he insists when he confronts Amanda's daughter with *his* annunciation. She is honored to learn this information, because she knows who Amanda is, not only from her reputation, but also because, ironically, they had run into each other on the Tulane campus.

Will turns and goes away, leaving her to handle the important fact of who her mother is—it is made quite obvious that she is a fragile personality who is much too dependent on her therapist—and, back in Fayetteville, Amanda is having her baby on Christmas Eve. The Annunciation motif has come full circle. But in a horrible instance of deus ex machina, Will is involved in a car accident that night on his way to Fayetteville, and the reader is led to believe he is killed. That is the end of novel. And a face-slapping ending it is, too. In fact, it is a cop-out ending, a cheap ending. The reader turns the last page expecting to find that Will and Amanda have worked things out, a fair and proper way for a novel to end. But instead, Gilchrist's emphasizes that the new baby, not Will, is the *most* important element of Amanda's new life—Will, who was only the "instrument" by which Amanda was given the child. This is truly an Annunciation scenario. (Readers who continue to follow Gilchrist's oeuvre in the order in which her novels and short-story collections were published will learn at a later point that Will was *not* killed that Christmas Eve, but that he came back to live in Fayetteville with Amanda and their son; but readers who read nothing more of Gilchrist's work of course never learn that information.)

So, ultimately, is Amanda's relationship with Will simply a clichéd relationship, the typical older woman and younger man situation? Cliché, perhaps, by its definition, by its outward appearance, if the individuals are removed *as* individuals from the equation. For knowing Amanda *as* the individual who forms as the novel progresses (and the same holds true to a lesser degree for Will), their relationship emerges from beneath the homogenizing veil of cliché to be real in its unique way. Amanda and Will dance with each other, both literally and figuratively. Figuratively they dance around their relationship, shoring up their own individual vulnerability now over here, now over there, trying not to place too much of a future spin on what is happening today. All the while, Amanda is trying to understand this entirely grown-up love for a man, a love she's never felt before.

The same kind of point-of-view problems found in her first collection of short stories—too abrupt, too whiplash—also occur throughout this novel. But the important thing for us to realize is that a long narrative can accommodate these too-quick point of view shifts, because they do not really break the reader's delicate concentration that is so necessary to feel the effectiveness of a short story. They do not threaten to turn the story into someone else's story, with a too-dizzying result. In fact, they do here in this novel what Gilchrist perhaps hopes they do in her short stories: they broaden character by casting different lights on them, allowing readers a multi-angle view.

Gilchrist's down-home, eloquent voice carries readers through this thoughtful novel as easily as driving in an open car on the smoothest blacktop road on a quiet, warm, summer night. Frances Taliaterro, writing a review of the novel in *Harper's*, found it "women's fiction par excellence" and a "surprisingly likeable novel."[25] But countering that positive criticism was novelist Rosellen Brown in *Saturday Review*. She took a lukewarm stand, averring that "Gilchrist's eagerly awaited first novel . . . is an unevenly compelling book by a talented short story writer who hasn't quite maneuvered the leap from short fiction to long."[26] Critic Jonathan Yardley went even farther in his lack of enthusiasm, calling the novel "flabby, narcissistic, and sophomoric."[27]

Chapter 4

Short Story Successes (*Victory over Japan, Drunk with Love*)

WITH A STRONG DEBUT IN THE SHORT STORY FORM with *In the Land of Dreamy Dreams* and a genuinely applaudable first novel, *The Annunciation*, Ellen Gilchrist quickly established her name. Her next two books were short story collections, *Victory over Japan,* which was published in 1984, and *Drunk with Love,* appearing in 1986. These two collections advanced her stature even further. "What comes through best is the infectious, languorous accent of the Delta," said one reviewer of *Victory over Japan*.[1] And critic Jonathan Yardley, dismissive of Gilchrist's novel *The Annunciation* nevertheless found that "at the end [of *Victory*] you have that satisfied, contented feeling only a good novel can give."[2] Also Gilchrist now gained a wider appreciation by the general reading public and the public librarian, the latter who purvey not only what the public wants, but what they know the reading public will enjoy. (*Victory over Japan* was listed on the 1984 Notable Books list, a yearly compilation of outstanding books for libraries chosen by the Notable Books Council, a committee of the American Library Association, and made up of a select group of librarians from across the country.)

In fact, *Victory over Japan* was awarded the prestigious National Book Award, particularly impressive for a collection of short stories, a fictional form typically considered the "junior partner" of the novel. There are 14 stories in *Victory over Japan,* and 13 in *Drunk with Love*. These 27 stories together testify to a sense of balance in creating short stories that are not only discrete but that are also partners with others in the collection, making, if not a perfectly seamless narrative, at least a solid, many-faceted one that offers a composite picture of lives that share similar backgrounds and crises.

Much of this sense of integration results from the frequent appearance, in both of these two collections, of Gilchrist's recurrent female characters. Rhoda Manning and Nora Jane Whittington were both introduced in Gilchrist's first short story collection, and Rhoda and Nora Jane reappear in many of the stories in the subsequent two collections.

Victory over Japan contains three Rhoda stories. The first two, "Victory over Japan," and "Music," are companion pieces to the trio of Rhoda-as-child stories—"Revenge," "1944," and "Perils of the Nile"—found in Gilchrist's first collection. The third Rhoda story in *Victory over Japan* is called "The Lower Garden District Free Gravity Mule Blight or Rhoda, a Fable," which is a sequel to "1957, a Romance," the story in *In the Land of Dreamy Dreams,* in which the character of Rhoda debuted.

The Rhoda in these three stories in *Victory* is the same Rhoda as in the four stories about her in the previous collection: that is, understandable and even likable as a young girl, but although as easy to understand, certainly not as easy to like as a teenager and as a young grown woman. The title story in *Victory* presents a good example of her nature as a little girl. It is set in a small town in Indiana during World War II (a return, of course, to the time and place of the three Rhoda-as-little-girl stories in *Dreamy Dreams*). The adult Rhoda is recalling when, in the third grade, a classmate of hers, a boy, had to undergo the painful series of injections that were necessary back then to prevent rabies. Watching Billy being escorted out of class every afternoon to go to the doctor cast a pall over the whole classroom. "Billy's shots had even taken the fun out of recess. Now we sat around on the fire escape and talked about rabies instead."[3] Gilchrist's childhood perspective is immaculate and unfaltering here; and in her description of Billy's lack of stature in the classroom, she demonstrates both incisiveness and humor in viewing life from the point of view of a child. Billy was "a small washed-out-looking boy that nobody paid any attention to until he got bit. He never talked to anybody. He could hardly even read. . . . No one would ever have picked him out to be the center of a rabies tragedy. He was more the type to fall in a well or get sucked down the drain at the swimming pool."[4] In other words, it was more likely that something mundane would befall Billy rather than something sympathetic and even slightly noble such as rabies.

Rhoda decides to interview Billy for the school paper, for she is the only third grader to have had something published in the school paper. Obviously her plan doesn't truly arise from genuine concern for Billy and his misfortune. Rhoda, we have learned, is Rhoda: always thinking of herself—in this case, of how she can make *herself* part of the Billy story. It is the biggest news of the moment at school, and Rhoda wants a role in it to make herself look good. But this is a perfectly understandable attitude in a headstrong, generally selfish child—and who would argue that most children *don't* fit that description? Rhoda tries everyone's, including the reader's, patience when she behaves this way as a teenager and young woman, but at this point at this age and time in her life, her ways of thinking and doing things are to be delighted in.

Later that day, the war intrudes into even the third grade, when a lady from the PTA comes to elicit the students' help in a paper drive. "We've licked the Krauts," she tells them in war-time lingo, "Now all we have left is the Japs."[5]

Rhoda immediately volunteers, and, just as spontaneously, she chooses Billy for her partner—but all for the effect of it, of course. Her mother is so proud that Rhoda chose Billy that she bakes her some cookies when she gets home that afternoon. Not one to suffer for lack of self-esteem even at this tender age, Rhoda insists, "I was getting to be more like my mother every day. My mother was a saint." Little Rhoda posits, "I bet this is the happiest day of her [my mother's] life."[6]

During the actual drive the following Saturday, Rhoda and Billy prove themselves very successful. On their last sweep down the street they come to a house where no one had been home before—"a house where old people live."[7] In another faultless expression of a child's perspective, Rhoda says, in reference to this particular house, "I had noticed old people were the ones who saved things."[8] In fact the man who comes to the door allows Rhoda and Billy to go get a stack of magazines in his basement—a gold mine in terms of the paper drive. But the magazines turn out to be full of naked people, and Rhoda and Billy dispose of them in the bushes and a ditch. Rhoda admonishes Billy to never speak to anyone about those dirty magazines.

But she did indeed write her article on Billy for the school paper, headlined with "Be On The Lookout For Mad Squirrel." Rhoda attempted to tell her mother about the magazines later in the summer, but unfortunately she'd chosen the wrong moment to bring it up. "Be quiet, Rhoda," her mother insisted, "we're listening to the news."[9] A big new bomb had been dropped on Japan, and, in another acute example of a child's perspective on things, Rhoda believes "Japan was sinking into the sea. Now the Japs had to surrender. Now they couldn't come to Indiana and stick bamboo up our fingernails. Now it would be all over and my father would come home."[10]

Rhoda's selfishness is allowable in someone in the third grade. In fact, her childish selfishness is ingratiating because it is so realistic; it injects an ironic but easy lovability into the young Rhoda. Her early developed, strong, and distinctive personality, and her healthy ego, almost demand selfishness as support. She is simply too young to be able to sustain good self-esteem without making everything in the world about *her*.

Contrarily, the teenage Rhoda, at least in the other two Rhoda stories in *Victory over Japan*, "Music" and "The Lower Garden District Free Gravity Mule Bight or Rhoda, a Fable" (is Gilchrist's typically clever, evocative use of titles simply too clumsy here?), has not only *not* outgrown her childish selfishness but, in fact, seems to have cultivated it to a higher degree. The result is a tiresome and even irritating Rhoda. "Music" is overlong (35 pages) for sustaining interest in Rhoda at age 14, five years older than in the previous story, for now she is obnoxious and stubborn, without the concomitant childhood charm. She's bored, too, but in turn she's boring for her family to be around. In the teenage Rhoda is a trait that will come to fruition in the later stories about young adult Rhoda: how much she exaggerates herself *to* herself and to others. As little as it is appreciated in the teenage Rhoda, it will be even less appreciated in the young adult version of her. But the *characterization* of Rhoda can never be argued against, can never be faulted—which is a major point to be stressed in discussing this particular story or *any* Rhoda story. Gilchrist creates Rhoda with a scrupulous, constant eye to an honest portrayal as she sees Rhoda in the various stages of her emotional development, whether Rhoda's actions are always admirable or not (most of them are, in fact, manipulative). This realism makes her understandable; and understanding a character is paramount, even when having to accept and overlook irritating sides (except in this particular story, which is *too* long for Rhoda to be *so* irritating without redeeming qualities as a balance).

In the first paragraph, the context of the story is quickly identified: "the summer her father dragged her off to Clay County, Kentucky, to make her stop smoking and acting like a movie star."[11] Her father—married, of course—is having an affair with a woman in Kentucky who lives close to the coalmines that are making Rhoda's father rich. As he is described—"deep down inside he believed there was nothing he couldn't do, even love two woman at once, even make Rhoda stop smoking"[12]—it is not difficult to see where Rhoda gets her large self-confidence and stubbornness. But though he fails with Rhoda, yet his failure to alter her is sympathetic. He finds his daughter offensive, particularly at one point when, wanting to leave Rhoda for the night with a local woman while he goes off to visit his lover, Rhoda refers to the woman with whom he wants her to stay as "poor white trash."[13]

"Haven't I taught you anything?"[14] he wonders aloud; then he throws quite a declaration in her face: "Your momma is a very stupid person, and I'm sorry I ever let her raise you."[15] Again, in the father we see the daughter: namely, right here, in their propensity for drama and exaggeration.

Left to her own devices while her father is away, and in the process of being driven to find a cigarette at any cost, Rhoda loses her virginity; and, despite Rhoda's premature crustiness and cynicism, this is a beautiful, heart-warming scene. Her father, correctly guessing what has transpired in his absence, is understandably furious; and he puts her on a plane the next morning, bound for home. The story ends 30 years later, with Rhoda having written a book about which her father is deeply embarrassed. Three decades later, she and he are still contentious: the parent-child picture carried away from this story is a lifetime of dueling (a conclusion corroborated again and again in the Rhoda stories involving her father that will appear in subsequent collections).

In "Lower Garden District," Rhoda is a young wife at basically the same time in her life as she was in "1957, a Romance" from *In the Land of Dreamy Dreams*. She is leaving her husband Jody; she plans to sell the house, get a job, and get a boyfriend, all in short and regular order. "Everything would fall into place. Jody would hang himself, and the will would still be made out in her favor, and she would quit her job and go live in New York."[16]

The Rhoda of this story has yet to shed the skin of immaturity. She is a married woman, and she still is imagining that the world revolves around her and is there to be manipulated to suit her. She has not really gotten past those school days back when she thrust herself into the middle of schoolmate Billy's tragic story of rabies. Specifically, then, this story is about how Rhoda has filed a false claim for her diamond ring, insisting to herself "All I'm doing is cheating an insurance company. It's the first time I ever stole anything in my life except that time in the fifth grade. Everybody gets to steal something sooner or later."[17]

This is the extent so far of Rhoda's maturity: entitlement and exemption. Her dishonesty actually grates less than her annoyingness in believing dishonesty is *fine* for her. As it turns out, the insurance company gives her close to five thousand dollars. "A day's work. At last, a real day's work."[18] So Rhoda believes, in her sense of self-delusion.

The irritation of Rhoda's immaturity and self-deceptiveness does not, ironically, lessen the lovely limpidness of Gilchrist's prose style. To encounter such a passage as this one about the sailing vacations Rhoda and her husband used to take in the Caribbean is to be reminded of it: "While somewhere ashore, down one of the dirt roads where Jody never let her go, oh, there Rhoda imagined real life was going on, a dark musky, musical real life, loud jump-ups she heard at night, hot black wildness going on and on into the night. . . ."[19]

At story's end Rhoda admits to the insurance agent that she committed fraud; but she also seduces him—retreating back into a man's arms for safety, despite her previous insistence, early in the story, on cultivating her newly found independence. The ambivalence Gilchrist's female protagonists often feel about freedom versus male attachments arises often; and the point to keep making vis-à-vis this issue is its *honesty*. "Ring true" is a cliché expression, but it has veracity when describing Rhoda and the other of Gilchrist's female characters.

Rhoda appears three times in the next short story collection, *Drunk with Love*: in "Nineteen Forty-One," "The Expansion of the Universe," and "Adoration." The first of this trio again focuses on Rhoda's dislocated girlhood in southern Indiana and Illinois during World War II, far removed—certainly in her adolescent view, at least—from the more comfortable circumstances she knew back in her native Mississippi. As the story opens, Rhoda is basically killing time, sitting on the sidewalk trying to start a fire with a magnifying glass, training the light beam on ants. Her father wants her to help entertain the banker's daughter, and Rhoda is stubbornly resisting having to do something she simply does not want to do. "I can't," she says, in finding what she believes is a good excuse, "I'm menstruating."[20]

Her father has a fit over Rhoda talking about such things—and talking about them so prematurely. He is joined by Rhoda's also incredulous but not as angry mother, and Rhoda says to them, showing off her rather mature sense of humor and certainly her already keen sense of manipulation, "'I've been doing it all morning. There's blood all over the sidewalk. Go look for yourself.' Actually, Rhoda spilled red Kool-Aid, which is what had drawn the ants. 'You can die if you aren't careful,' she continued. 'Anything can happen when you menstruate.'"[21]

In the end Rhoda is forced to entertain the banker's daughter (at horse-riding, as a matter of fact), and, Rhoda being Rhoda, which means ever ready to exploit a situation to suit her own advantage, she reminds herself of this girl's probable affluence. "She might have a playhouse or a chauffeur or anything."[22] But Rhoda takes a fall from her horse, and her resentment against her brother for simply being a boy, and thus being allowed activities that are proscribed for her because of her gender (an attitude she has made quite manifest before, in "Revenge" from *In the Land of Dreamy Dreams*, a story, it will be remembered, about the broad-jump pit), surfaces here in this story when Rhoda regains consciousness in her bed. She accuses her brother of trying to kill her by not saddling her horse properly so he could inherit everything their parents have.

Her father dismisses her childish insistence with a simple, "Come on son,"[23] and putting his arm around Rhoda's brother, and, expressing the male bonding from which Rhoda is so sorely excluded, tossing over his shoulder as he leads her brother from the room the most condescending thing Rhoda could hear, "Let your mother take care of you."[24]

The story ends with Rhoda's wish that the horse she'd ridden now be killed: the child-Rhoda capable of at least expressing awful vengefulness. Vengefulness sits compatibly with selfishness and manipulativeness in children: again, we come face to face with Gilchrist's accuracy and authenticity in understanding children.

Rhoda's resentment at being excluded from the company of men, especially her sense of forced exile outside the bonds connecting her father and her brothers, will be a sentiment she carries into middle age, to be witnessed in many forthcoming stories; this sense of exclusion will also come to include the relationship her own sons have with her father.

In "The Expansion of the Universe," Rhoda, at age 13, has indeed begun menstruating, which she had been "dying" to do, fearing she "would be the last person in Southern Illinois to menstruate."[25] In this story, then, as in the previous one, Rhoda's family is still dislocated from Mississippi during the days when World War II raged—in the outside world, that is. As pleased as Rhoda is about the advent of her womanhood, she appears blasé when she tells her mother about it; she "tossed the information over her shoulder on her way out the door."[26]

Thoughtlessly, "then she was gone, as Rhoda was always going, leaving her mother standing in a doorway or the middle of a room with her jaw clenched and her nails digging into her palms and everything she had believed all her life in question."[27]

Rhoda's friend Lelia tells Rhoda of the pleasures of "dry-fucking," and Rhoda is both excited and appalled. She asks her mother about what it was like being pregnant, and her mother uses this as an opportunity to impart a little "editorial" commentary to her daughter in the form of some frank information. "You came too fast," she tells her. "You tore me up coming out. Like everything else you've ever done. You never could wait for anything."[28]

Rhoda is then informed that the family is going to be moving again, which, apparently, they have done several times before. But right now Rhoda's mind is on one thing only—that her older boyfriend is coming home from college for the weekend, "and then he would be there and she would be in his arms and life would begin."[29] By chronological age Rhoda is still a teenager, of course, but in her own mind, *of course*, she has arrived at womanhood—but, interestingly, as a "woman" needing a man for "life" to begin.

Bob, her boyfriend, does indeed come home for the weekend, and he gives Rhoda his pin to wear, and tells her he loves her. Then he's gone, back to college; and Rhoda is left "trying to hold the day inside so it would never end."[30] But the fact that the family is relocating to Kentucky quickly becomes something Rhoda cannot ignore. Her protests to her father result in only his insistence that she is "a little silly girl."[31] Thus there is nothing Rhoda can do about this move but give in; but, of course, even in her acquiescence, she must have the last word, which is the last line of the story: "It better be a big house. It had better be the biggest house in that goddamn town."[32]

Five years of Rhoda's life have passed when she is encountered again, in the story "Adoration." (Is it any surprise that a story involving self-involved Rhoda would have that title?) Rhoda is now 19, married, and pregnant—and her pregnancy is making her ill. She lives in Atlanta with the young man she had married after having known him for only one week; and Rhoda is putting him through school. Has Rhoda turned sacrificial and generous? Not really, because there is evidence in this story that she still can manipulate her father into giving her anything she asks him for.

Because her pregnancy is so troublesome—lots of bleeding—her husband takes her to her mother in Alabama. On the way Rhoda dreams of her baby—she definitely wants a boy (again, not surprising that she would desire another man in her life, to both rely on and take advantage of!)—and she dreams of his being a swimmer. But her family doctor back in Alabama is not certain she isn't in the process of miscarrying, about which Rhoda experiences mixed emotions: one minute happy she isn't having a baby, the next minute telling her doctor "I like it inside of me."[33] She dreams again of a baby boy; and in the same dream her father appears, surrounded by ladies, and Rhoda observes to herself in her dream that he "was never cold to them."[34] Contradictorily, in real life, he was indeed often that way to *her*.

So she does have the baby, the boy she wanted; and he makes Rhoda and her husband almost happy. She gets pregnant again, and she goes to the doctor quite often "because he was the best-looking man in Atlanta."[35] (Rhoda will always be Rhoda!) She is still being taken care of financially, even from long distance, by her parents.

The story now flashes ahead several years, and a 26-year-old Rhoda and her husband live in Kansas City, Kansas. On her birthday she and her husband, both drunk, conceive another baby, and Rhoda has a keen sense of the very second of its conception. As she goes to sleep that night, she figures this son, *this* male out of all the males in her life, will be the ultimate compliment to her. "This is the one who will swim the channel for me."[36] Rhoda is consistent in her conceitedness, constantly assuming the world revolves around her. The collection *Drunk with Love* certainly imparts that distinct taste of her. Will she ever change? Only further stories in subsequent collections will tell.

But another popular Gilchrist recurrent character also appears in these two collections, *Victory over Japan* and *Drunk with Love*. Nora Jane Whittington is her name, and she was introduced in the hilarious story "The Famous Poll at Jody's Bar" in Gilchrist's first story collection, *In the Land of Dreamy Dreams*. In that story Nora Jane robbed a bar in her hometown of New Orleans to get money to join her boyfriend Sandy in California. *Victory over Japan* presents a two-story sequence, picking up the story of Nora Jane from that point, and carrying her adventures farther.

In "Jade Buddhas, Red Bridges, Fruits of Love," Nora Jane goes to California to meet Sandy, having written to him that she was coming; but, understandably disappointing to her, he's not waiting for her at the airport. She takes a cab to his address, all of this adventure serving as quite an education for her, since, as she informs the cab driver, "It's the first time I've been farther west than Alexandria [Louisiana]."[37] Sandy isn't home so, ever resourceful, Nora Jane breaks a window to let herself in, only to discover evidence of Sandy's infidelity. Nora Jane is uncertain what her next step should be. She ponders the insignificance of our individual stories in the overall scheme of the universe, and, even though this realization and acceptance lasts for only a brief moment in the story, it nevertheless subtly establishes the fundamental difference between the personalities of Nora Jane and Rhoda: the latter is certainly more experienced and worldly, but she has yet to digest and process all her advantages into a mature sense of herself as *not* being the center of everyone's universe.

On the other hand, Nora Jane's inherent consideration of other people is observed in a small but telling incident: while still in Sandy's house, she eats a candy bar she had brought with her, but she doesn't just drop the wrapper—instead, she puts it back in her pack, for she "never littered anything. So far in her life she had not thrown down a single gum wrapper."[38] Such environmental and social sensitivity would not be expected from Rhoda.

Nora Jane rents a room near the Berkeley campus, and she soon experiences a not uncommon feature of California life, earthquakes, four of them in fact, all occurring during the course of her first week. (After the first one, she meets a Chinese couple who are also living in the house—who will appear again in the next Nora Jane story, and who will play an important role.) The following morning, Nora Jane goes out and buys a stage pistol from a theatrical supply store, shades of her recent past coming back to color her present, making it not difficult to guess how she intends to get some money in her hands.

A white space now sets off a new section of the story, and the point of view changes to a new character, Freddy Harwood. Despite Gilchrist's previous exercises of it, with negative effect, *this* point of view shift only *enhances* the story, and does not derail it. That at this point the story now becomes Freddy's story as well allows Gilchrist to bring in yet another rich character; from this point on, in any Nora Jane story, wherever she is, Freddy will be there as well. He is a strong character—the strongest male character Gilchrist has yet to create—who at first functions as an effective counterpoint to Nora Jane, throwing her true grit and fortitude into sharp relief. Then he becomes an even more vigorous supporter and ally of hers. Freddy's presence as well as his actions toward Norah Jane increase the reader's understanding of Nora Jane's nature and deepen the reader's appreciation of her quirky, but basically *good,* nature. Freddy's presence also heightens this particular story's dramatic conflict, as he will do in every story in which he appears.

Freddy owns "the biggest and least profitable"[39] bookstore in northern California. As already indicated, he is one of Gilchrist's most rounded and sympathetically drawn male characters; and an important aspect of him comes across very quickly by way of Gilchrist's ability to summarize a character's salient traits and toss some humor and satire into the quick mix: "He knew dozens of writers. Writers adored him. . . . He even read their books. He went that far. He actually read their books."[40] Freddy has recently been named one of the Bay area's most eligible bachelors, and he has girlfriends everywhere. He is in the pay of his rich grandmother (perhaps not his noblest trait). Freddy and Nora Jane cross paths at a café, where they engage in conversation, and he invites her to his bookstore—where she pulls out the stage gun and attempts to rob him! But Freddy reveals himself to be a better con than Nora Jane; he begins reciting one of his favorite poems, a trick he's used with women before. "He had seen hardhearted graduate students pull off their sweaters by the third line."[41] And, to be sure, his recitation literally disarms Nora Jane. Off they go together to get something to eat; they begin seeing each other, and Nora Jane gets a job at an art gallery. But soon her boyfriend Sandy (she had stolen money in order to come to California to see him) finds her, after returning home from Colorado.

Not surprisingly, Sandy's arrival on the scene gives Freddy no pleasure; but Sandy's advent casts telling light on Freddy's importance in Nora Jane's life, not so much as a foil, but more as a role model for her for strength of character and fortitude in accomplishing what one needs to get done in life—which, for Freddy right now, is having Nora Jane.

Freddy ups the ante by giving Nora Jane a brand new convertible. Over Nora Jane's objections to taking a gift so significant, Freddy sways her with his additional charm, charisma, and smooth talk, explaining to her, "Don't look like that, Nora Jane. It's okay to have a car. Cars are all right. They satisfy our need for strong emotions."[42]

But even when ultimately agreeing to accept the car, Nora Jane insists she won't be driving over a bridge because her fear of them is much too intense. But Freddy counters with the insistence that one can't live in the Bay area and not cross bridges. Freddy, the consummate persuader, compels her to change her mind with these elegant words: "Listen to me a minute. I want to tell you about these bridges. People like us didn't build these bridges, N.J. People like Teddy Roosevelt and Albert Einstein and Aristotle built those bridges. . . . The Golden Gate is so overbuilt you could stack cars two deep on it and it wouldn't fall."[43]

So she does it—takes her new car over a bridge—the Oakland Bridge. Thus she is symbolically crossing from her old, insecure life back in New Orleans to a new, more certain life here in California, almost as if she were a pioneer from the East in the early or mid-1900s, now having come West to find a better future.

In the longish story "The Double Happiness Bun," Nora Jane is pregnant and is being pursued by a marriage-minded Freddy. Nora Jane is not about to be persuaded to do something she doesn't feel like doing—her position taken not out of sheer stubbornness (a posture Rhoda would assume) but because she is wise and mature enough to see a wrong path for what it is. She won't marry Freddy because she doesn't love him—it's as simple as that.

"How could you make love to someone like last night if you didn't love them? I don't believe it,"[44] Freddy whines to her—seeming *naive*, but Freddy, so the reader learns very quickly, is just as wise as Nora Jane.

Nora Jane's refusal to marry Freddy is compounded by the fact that she's not certain whether he or Sandy is the father of her unborn child (she had recently slept with Sandy, too). Sandy, predictably, is involved in a shady business deal, and he wants to draw Nora Jane in. With this proposition, the contrast between what Freddy and Sandy have to offer Nora Jane could not be more stark: Freddy has money and a legitimate business, Sandy has very little money and is never on the up-and-up when it comes to making some.

Nora Jane is not self-destructive, as Rhoda often can be—this being an important trait of Nora Jane's as well as a significant difference in the two characters. Nora Jane's survival instinct now comes into consequential play; it informs her that she needs to be rid of Sandy. The Chinese couple who live in Nora Jane's building, who were introduced in the previous story, suggest that perhaps she is having *two* babies—"like Double Happiness Bun. One for each father."[45]

Freddy doesn't want anyone knowing of Nora Jane's uncertainty about the identity of the father; and Nora Jane's reaction is laudable. "I've never been ashamed of anything I've done in my life, and I'm not about to start being ashamed now."[46] She further underscores her strength of character and independence when, upon hearing an art critic talking snootily at the art gallery where she works, she turns in her resignation, summarizing her reasoning as "I'm going to have a baby and I don't want it floating around inside me listening to people say nasty things about other peoples' paintings."[47] Nora Jane's strong streak of self-preservation obviously extends to protecting her unborn child as well, and this extension of her propensity for preservation to include the people she comes to love will be one of the most satisfying qualities Nora Jane continues to exhibit and refine in subsequent stories about her.

Nora Jane plans to get a job at a day-care center. "I'll live on whatever they pay me. That's one thing Sandy taught me. You don't have to do what they want you to do if you don't have to have their stuff. It was worth living with him just to learn that."[48] (Here another difference between Nora Jane and Rhoda can be seen: Nora Jane's ability—or *humility*—to learn from her experiences, even if, in retrospect, they turned out to be mistakes.)

In the story I discussed before this one, Nora Jane conquered her fear of bridges. At this point, after quitting her job, Nora Jane sails off aimlessly in her convertible and finds herself on the Richmond–San Rafael Bridge. An earthquake occurs, and the approaches to the bridge are destroyed, leaving Nora Jane and several other motorists stranded out on the bridge. Next to her is a woman in a station wagon full of screaming children; a very adult Nora Jane takes charge and settles the children down with a song until they can be rescued off the bridge. (The good quality of Nora Jane's voice is information we learned in the first Nora Jane story, "The Famous Poll at Jody's Bar," in *In the Land of Dreamy Dreams*.)

In the two stories in *Victory over Japan* in which Nora Jane stars, we found her so likable that we can't help but admire her, specifically for her strength, spunk, and not-ruthless ambition. She is not overwhelmed and undermined by her own ego and selfishness and boredom like Rhoda is. It will be interesting, then, to proceed to the one story featuring Nora Jane in *Drunk with Love*—which is the title story—and to find out whether these characteristics hold true.

The story "Drunk with Love" is one of the best stories in the collection. From a technical point of view, it is immaculate: tight, clean, striking a strong punch, with not a flaccid passage in the whole narrative. In terms of characterization, Nora Jane and Freddy sail before the reader with all flags flying. They are acutely drawn individuals for whom great reader empathy is not only possible but also *impossible* not to feel. For someone who has never read a Nora Jane story before, this one is not only accessible and understandable, but it also serves as an enticement to read more stories about her; and it makes a rich contribution to the continuing saga of Nora Jane for readers who have enjoyed meeting her before.

Nora Jane and Freddy are found where they were left in the second of the two Nora Jane stories in *Victory over Japan*, "The Double Happiness Bun": specifically, Freddy is in a tizzy over Nora Jane's being pregnant and his not knowing whether he is the father, and Nora Jane's being rescued off the Richmond–San Rafael Bridge after an earthquake. Now in this story, Freddy is in his bookstore when the earthquake hits. Fleeing into the street, he is flagged down to help rescue two little boys from a burning building. He helps, but he has to be hospitalized afterward with burnt hands; the press proclaims him a hero for his bravery.

Nora Jane rushes to his bedside as soon as she gets back into the city from being stranded on the bridge. There she is proclaimed a heroine by the woman with the carload of children whom Nora Jane had entertained and calmed, and who had come with her to the hospital to find Freddy. Freddy is adamant that Nora Jane marry him; he doesn't want her to take the test that can determine whether he is the father of her unborn child but, instead, just to hurry up and marry him. At any rate, Nora Jane is greatly moved by his tenderness. She tells him on his hospital bed that she loves him, but she retracts her statement upon his release. Freddy responds with, "You don't have to love me, Nora Jane. As long as that baby belongs to me."[49] This shift in his attitude concerning the baby's true paternity is left a little gray, a little too unclear—no, it is *too* contradictory, going beyond Gilchrist's usually defensible practice of occasionally, and appropriately, showing the natural ambivalence in people toward certain situations and conditions, which is part of her formula for creating realism in characters and sharing the sense of their honesty.

In an uncommon moment of self-doubt, the usually confident Nora Jane wonders, "Why would anybody like that [like Freddy] want to like me anyway?"[50]

She has the amniocentesis, which indicates the presence of two fetuses. Nora Jane's honesty, when she continues to insist to Freddy the twins are probably not his, is an ethical attitude and action; how easy it would be for a less honorable young woman, pregnant and without much in the way of prospects, to marry the rich and handsome—and now heroic—Freddy, regardless of the true paternity of her children. Unlike Rhoda, Nora Jane refuses to exploit every situation available to her to her own advantage.

Now the story breaks into a second part that, in its first pages, sketches in Freddy's background. This is, fortunately, not one of Gilchrist's problematic point-of-view deviations in that it does not blindside the reader with a mid-paragraph shift to another character's perspective. Rather, in this case, the technique meaningfully brings in an important character's side of events. Within this same section, it is observed that Sandy, too, wants Nora Jane—not to marry him, for Sandy is not especially taken with permanence in life, but as his live-in girlfriend. Sandy has been experiencing some growth in maturity, "beginning to see that some of the things he had done might actually be affecting the lives of other people, especially and specifically Nora Jane."[51] He informs Nora Jane that he loves her, and, taking her in his arms, he discovers that "the old magic was as good as new."[52] He essentially surrenders to her, saying "I've had all I can take of loneliness. You can call the shots. You tell me what you want and I'll deliver."[53]

Nora Jane is being asked to choose between two men, and that places her in, yes, an emotional dilemma, but also in a position of strength, control, and bargaining power. But certainly Nora Jane will not exploit the situation to satisfy only her own selfish needs, as Rhoda would do in this situation. The story ends in what on a surface level seems hokey, but poignancy and humor nevertheless shine through. Nora Jane's two fetuses are having a "conversation" in her womb:

"'Nice night tonight.'

'I wish it could always be the same. She's always changing. Up and down. Up and down.'

'Get used to it. We'll be there soon.'

'Let's don't think about it.'

'You're right. Let's be quiet.'

'Okay.'"[54]

Regardless of the story's ending, the point of the piece is how Nora Jane has renewed the reader's affection for her; in fact, she makes it difficult not to wish to meet her again soon.

But until that time arrives—which, of course, it will—in four stories in the collection *Victory over Japan* and in one story in *Drunk with Love*, another one of Gilchrist's recurrent characters is introduced and developed: Traceleen, whose job it always is to narrate—and comment on—the exploits of her boss, Crystal Manning, who thus becomes another Gilchrist recurrent character. Crystal is Rhoda's cousin, and Traceleen is Crystal's black maid and nurse for the baby from Crystal's second marriage. Traceleen is devoted to her employer, but her outspoken views of events involving Crystal nonetheless paint a picture of her employer as sharing character traits with Rhoda: Crystal's spirit of independence, like Rhoda's, is actually rooted in selfishness and self-centeredness. Traceleen is easily appreciated as the central intelligence in Crystal's household from whom the closest thing to truth about Crystal and her generally chaotic life will emanate. This function is, of course, the most creative aspect of the Traceleen/Crystal stories: that is,

Traceleen is a kind and generous soul, who simply tells it like she sees it. Her honesty of observation, untainted by any meanness, is the brush by which the provocative Crystal is painted, warts and all.

In the sequence of Traceleen stories appearing in *Victory over Japan*— "Miss Crystal's Maid Traceleen, She's Talking, She's Telling Everything She Knows," "Traceleen's Telling a Story Called 'A Bad Year'," "Traceleen's Diary," and "Traceleen, She's Still Talking"—events in Crystal's life are related as Lucy Ricardo–type escapades from Traceleen's more grounded Ethel Mertz-type sensibilities and point of view. Gilchrist reserves a humorous voice for these stories, as well as for the kind of episodes Traceleen gives witness to (as in the first story in the sequence): "The worst thing that ever happened to Miss Crystal happened at a wedding. It was her brother-in-law's wedding. He was marrying this girl, her daddy was said to be the richest man Memphis. The Weisses were real excited about it. As much money as they got I guess they figure they can always use some more."[55]

So off they all go to Memphis to the wedding of Crystal's brother-in-law, the brother of her husband, Manny. Traceleen is, naturally, put in charge of taking care of Crystal's and Manny's little girl, Crystal Anne. As the wedding party leaves New Orleans and flies to Memphis, Crystal is all over the bridegroom's friend Owen. "She's in such a good mood," Traceleen says about Crystal, in her tendency for understatement. "I haven't seen her like that in a long time."[56] But she overhears Manny's admonition to Crystal, "Let's just remember this is Joey's wedding and try to act right."[57] Traceleen admits she feels "sorry for him sometimes. He's always having to police everything. Come from being a lawyer, I guess."[58]

It is clear, then, that Crystal has not only a wandering eye, but also a habit of getting into trouble. In this case, as it soon turns out, the trouble stems from Crystal's overly fond attention paid to Owen. The strange result is a tussle between Crystal and Manny, and Crystal's falling down the stairs, and for two months now, she has been hospitalized. As Traceleen observes, "Mr. Manny. He's got her where he wants her now, hasn't he? Any day when he gets off to work he can just drive to Touro and there she is, right where he left her, laying in bed, waiting for him to get there."[59]

That is certainly one way to have his wife's independence and self-assertion (and trouble making) curtailed. But in the end, Manny, along with Crystal's grown son from her first marriage, King, springs her from the hospital and takes her home. "Mr. Manny and King are so proud of themselves they have forgotten they are enemies."[60]

In the second Traceleen story, "Traceleen's Telling a Story Called 'A Bad Year'," the narrator's ever-appealing, yarn-spinning voice relates an even more entertaining yarn. This tale is about King, Crystal's son from her first marriage. It seems Crystal was involved in publishing a literary magazine, and her partner, a famous poet by the name of Mr. Alter (who strikes Traceleen as "the prettiest white man I ever did see in my life,"[61] and whose last name is a not-too-subtle allusion to his capacity to be an agent of change), comes to stay with Crystal and Manny one whole spring; and then he goes home and kills himself—an act that no one, including Traceleen, could understand. But the most distressed is King, who is only 14, "just the age for adoring someone."[62] When Mr. Alter shoots himself, King runs off to a hippie commune.

Crystal's father finally finds him, accomplishing what hired detectives failed to do. When King is brought back home, Crystal's brother, Phelan—whom we have not seen the last of, for he will be encountered again in later Traceleen/Crystal stories—literally gets hold of him and cuts off his hair, which upsets Crystal, who bears no great fondness for her brother in the first place. The upshot is that King runs away again, and he's gone for weeks.

Crystal is beside herself. Traceleen sees her aging right before her eyes. But Traceleen sees everything in balance. "They're some people in the world, seem like they're just meant to be more trouble than other people. Demand more, cause more trouble and cause more goodness, too. Someone's got to love and care for them. Got to study them, so we see how things are made to happen."[63]

But King finally returns home, and all is well.

The next Traceleen story, "Traceleen's Diary," is a charming yarn concerning the time when Crystal is determined to bring an end to the goings-on in a New Orleans bordello. And the last in the Traceleen sequence, "Traceleen, She's Still Talking," is an elaborately involved story centered on Crystal's brother, Phelan, who purchases a big Mercedes in Germany and has it shipped to New Orleans; from there Crystal is supposed to drive it to Phelan's ranch in Texas. The ensuing adventure strains plot credibility, but because the wonderful raconteur Traceleen is the one narrating it—and how she cherishes a good story to tell—the reader can only surrender and sit back to enjoy every odd turn this story takes.

Traceleen charms again in her one story found in the collection *Drunk with Love*, "Traceleen at Dawn." It is, in Traceleen's always to-the-point words, "the story of how Miss Crystal stopped drinking."[64] There is certainly joy to be taken in this Traceleen story, as in all the Traceleen stories. But Gilchrist also writes effective short stories that do *not* feature recurrent characters. A good case in point is "The Gauzy Edge of Paradise" in *Victory over Japan*. This is an inviting story, even an exciting one, about a trio of thoroughly enjoyable characters, even in their one-time-only appearance in Gilchrist's fiction. It proves difficult to resist reading farther on into a story that begins this way: "The only reason Lanier and I went to the coast to begin with was to lose weight. We didn't know we were going to have a ménage à trois with Sandor. We didn't even know Sandor was coming down there."[65]

Diane, the narrator, and her best friend, Lanier, live in Jackson, Mississippi, and both are secretaries to state legislators. They take a dieting trip to Diane's mother's beach house, but they are instructed to also pick up Diane's cousin, Sandor, who is flying into Pensacola. Diane explains him to Lanier as her gorgeous cousin who had wanted to be a movie star in California but who had a nervous breakdown over it.

So, per their instructions, Diane and Lanier pick Sandor up at the airport, and Lanier certainly likes what she sees. "You could hear her pull her stomach in."[66] At Sandor's suggestion, the three of them begin barhopping. They drink on top of the diet pills they've been taking. The possibility of a three-way sexual encounter is brought up—Diane insisting it was Lanier's idea. But out of the blue, the taxi driver who'd brought them to their hotel is standing at the door of their room with a gun in his hand. He robs them, leaving them tied up; and when they finally do arrive at the beach house, Diane thinks about her future dieting in a more fatalistic, but ironically more realistic way. "Good girls would press their elegant rib cages against their beautiful rich athletic husbands. Passionate embraces would ensue. I would be lying on a bed drinking chocolate milkshakes."[67]

This story is an entertaining example of Gilchrist's propensity for—and ability at—mixing humor with violence. She combines these two elements in the brief confines of the short story so unsubtly, yet so smoothly and realistically, that she elicits a simultaneous gulp of surprise and a tear of laughter from the reader. Gilchrist's handling of violence is consistently appropriate when she uses it; when she has it rear its graphic head, it can be shocking, dismaying, and jolting, but it is always just as organic to the story as violence is organic to contemporary society.

Gilchrist's violence is never gratuitous, as it can be in the fiction of Joyce Carol Oates, and it is never employed as it is in the fiction of Flannery

O'Connor, posing moral questions about good and evil and a punitive God. In Gilchrist's fiction, violence is never overplayed, never overly burdensome to either the story or the reader. She never insists that violence is the *primary* feature of today's world. In her fiction, her eye is mostly on how people make relationships work with family, friends, and lovers, with violence being a part of the equation when there is not only an appropriate, but almost *obligatory* need for it, as when showing the depths of Tom's personal despair in the story "Rich" (in *In the Land of Dreamy Dreams*) or how "let-loose" behavior can leave one vulnerable to violence as depicted in the otherwise amusing story just discussed, "The Gauzy Edge of Paradise."

In these two short story collections, *Victory over Japan* and *Drunk with Love*, Gilchrist proves her continued, even enhanced, mastery of the form. In fact, *Victory over Japan* is not only the strongest of her four books up to that point in her career, it has remained her best short story collection *to date*. The implication is not, of course, that she has declined in effectiveness since then; the point is simply that, until any further collection establishes otherwise, this collection—on the whole, that is—still stands as Gilchrist's definitive statement in the short story form.

By way of a review of her practice as a short story writer, it must admitted that she remains guilty of annoying point-of-view problems, continuing to make too many little abrupt shifts that come more as distractions to the reader than as heightening of the plot or deepening of characterization. But fortunately, in these last two collections she is able to break away from using inner paragraph jolts of point-of-view change to use instead the much more helpful white-space technique when refocusing the point of view in big chunks of text. Because she handles *that* technique so well, it does indeed have enhancement value.

Gilchrist has the art of the compelling opening down to a science, and that is important in making the short story form not only its most effective, but also most distinct from other literary forms. Admirable too is her instinct for appropriate, fluid, even rhythmic mixing and matching of summary and exposition—of describing a person or situation in the briefest but most telling of detail, and then breaking the story out into flinty, revealing dialogue and personal interaction between characters.

In a review of *Drunk With Love* in the *Los Angeles Times,* Meg Wolizer, herself an esteemed fiction writer, brings up an interesting point about this collection (and by implication about *all* short story collections): "What's missing here is a thread of commonality running through all the stories.

Instead, we have a variety of quirky characters leading all sorts of dissimilar lives."[68] That statement begs the question, what is wrong with a variety of quirky characters leading all sorts of dissimilar lives? The thing is, to claim that a short story collection has no strong thematic link among all the stories is an easy lob for a critic to throw. It is quick and ready criticism—but often invalid.

The truth of the matter is that story collections do not necessarily need "a thread of commonality." Most collections of short stories are just that: a collection, not a novel-in-stories. If a book is indeed a novel-in-stories, then it should be billed as such and then, yes, the stories-as-chapters will need strong linkage. But the real issue here is that, even when critics find a story collection lacking if it does not boast an obvious connection of all of its parts, the reading public may not. The general reading public reads a collection of short stories as a sampling of the author's work in that form. They do not necessarily expect a thread of commonality; they do not miss one if it is not present, and they probably would not recognize one—at least a subtle one—if it were there. And that is not to cast disparagement on the general reading public. It is simply a statement that, critics' views aside, Gilchrist's readers love her quirky characters and their dissimilar lives and would seem far less likely than critics to complain that there is no obvious thematic connection between the stories in one of her collections. The connection is that they are all by *her*, and that is good enough.

But even the generally respected *Victory over Japan* attracted some negative responses, typified by this review in the *Christian Science Monitor*, in which the reviewer posed this question: "Why are some of the stories such a pleasure, and others so unsatisfying? Her [Gilchrist's] style has a lot to do with it. . . . It's a style well-suited to wit and surprise but ill-equipped for expansion and reflection. . . . It's hard to care about Nora Jane . . . or about Miss Crystal. . . . Their mistakes have no consequence and therefore seem trivial."[69]

Chapter 5

Slight of Hand
(The Anna Papers, I Cannot Get You Close Enough)

ANNA HAND, A FAMOUS WRITER AND COUSIN to Rhoda Manning and Crystal Manning, is yet another one of Gilchrist's recurrent characters, although her recurrences are less frequent than Rhoda's or Crystal's. Anna Hand is the protagonist of Gilchrist's next book and second novel *The Anna Papers*, which was published in 1988. Actually Anna Hand made her first appearance, however briefly, in the short story "Looking Over Jordan" in the collection *Victory over Japan*; and, further, she made another "exposure"— this time more fully—in the concluding story in *Drunk with Love*, "Anna, Part I." Jumping ahead two books after *The Anna Papers*, a trio of novellas called *I Cannot Get you Close Enough* (1990) portrays additional incidences in the life of Anna Hand as well as in the lives of other members of the Hand family introduced in *The Anna Papers*.

Consequently, a discussion of the whole Anna Hand sequence—all at once, in other words—is called for. Together, the Anna Hand material—two short stories, a novel, and three novellas—sets up interesting comparisons and contrasts in how successfully and not so successfully Gilchrist is in command of her "Hand" material. Therefore, it will be necessary to temporarily set aside a strictly chronological approach to Gilchrist's oeuvre. Between the novel *The Anna Papers* and the novella collection *I Cannot Get You Close Enough* there appeared, in 1989, a short story collection, *Light Can Be Both Wave and Particle*; and this collection contains no stories about Anna or her family. A "right" exists, then, permitting a momentary postponement of discussing it.

In "Looking over Jordan" in *Victory over Japan,* Anna Hand takes her inaugural turn on the Gilchrist stage, and for this auspicious debut Gilchrist has created a beautiful story, exquisite and faultless in its execution. Now admittedly, Anna Hand is more of an off-stage character in this story; that said, the story is very much *about* her, or at least the "threat" of her.

Lady Margaret Sarpie lives in New Orleans, but today is a bad day for her: disagreeable weather, rude bathroom scales, and her cousin, Devoie, is staying on for an additional week. And if those things weren't difficult enough, the phone keeps ringing. When Lady Margaret answers it, no one is even there. "Lady Margaret's father had been a brigadier general in the army. People weren't supposed to call Lady Margaret and hang up. They weren't even supposed to look at her unless she told them to."[1]

Lady Margaret calls her mother to see if she can use her mother's beach house to escape the harassment for a few days. As it turns out, Lady Margaret has negatively reviewed in the local newspaper the new novel by the famous writer Anna Hand, because of the unflattering images—"attacks"—that Lady Margaret felt Anna gave New Orleans; and she fears the phone calls are coming either from Anna or from people who are irritated at what Lady Margaret wrote. Lady Margaret and her cousin, Devoie, go off to the beach house, even though someone is already staying there: Armand, a family relative. In a typical abrupt point of view shift—but in this case, because it has the effect of layering the story rather than *derailing* it, it works fine—the reader is whisked out to the beach house ahead of Lady Margaret, to find Armand ensconced with a woman he more or less just picked up—none other than the famous Anna Hand, herself in New Orleans on a publicity tour. Anna has spent the night, and she wants to go back into town to get the rest of her things from the hotel and then be taken to the airport; but she informs Armand that she wants to check whether the local newspaper has reviewed her book. "God only knows who they'll give it to. They gave the last one to a Jesuit. Can you believe it? He said I made unjustified attacks on the Church. Unjustified. Isn't that wonderful?"[2]

What really *is* wonderful is the showdown between Anna and Lady Margaret, when the latter arrives from town and the former is still in "residence"—she and Armand not having departed yet to get Anna to her afternoon flight. Lady Margaret, when she gets out of the car and steps up to the house, notices a hat on the swing—and senses she has seen that hat before, which, indeed, she has, since Anna Hand is wearing it in the author photo on the jacket of the book Lady Margaret just *negatively* reviewed. Inside, Lady Margaret comes face to face with a woman who, after Lady Margaret introduces herself, introduces *herself* as Anna Hand. In the face of Lady Margaret's obvious and understandable shock, Anna asks, "Is something wrong? Are you all right?" But, fortunately for Lady Margaret, Anna didn't hear her name when she spoke it; and when Anna asks her to repeat it, Lady Margaret stalls. She now wonders whether this whole arrangement has been a joke played on her by Armand.

After Armand and Anna have gone, Lady Margaret realizes that "the world is full of danger. Anything can happen to anyone at any time."[3] She attempts a sort of reconciling communion with Anna by finishing the cup of coffee Anna had been drinking. But even this doesn't wash away Lady Margaret's feeling of unease, so there is really nothing else for her to do but conclude "Well, to hell with it. I didn't do anything wrong. I just wrote what I thought."[4]

This amusing story, told concisely and precisely, affords a first sighting of Anna Hand—famous, and powerful in her fame. Almost awesome. The opportunity to encounter her again, this time more extensively, is afforded in the story "Anna, Part I," from the collection *Drunk with Love*. This is, in the simplest of terms, a story of an affair: Anna's. The story has intrigue; it even unsettles; yet with a sense of completeness, it is a richly realized portrait of a self-possessed but believably conflicted personality.

The first line takes the reader to a new geographic place for Gilchrist: the Carolinas. It is established on the first page that today is a day of great consequence for Anna Hand: she is forsaking being a "fool" and returning to her writing career. The source of her foolishness is that she's been in New York City having an affair with a married man, wasting "ten goddamn months in the jaws of love."[5] Back in North Carolina now, Anna feels confident in making good on her promise to her editor that she will have a book of stories completed in a few months.

Once she has organized a supportive nest around herself for her creativity to grow, Anna sits down to write, and she decides to write about the married man with whom she had the affair in New York. This leads to the story's second part, a flashback to New York and her relationship with the "tall red-haired baby doctor."[6] As she enters into an affair with him, she advises herself *not* to. Nonetheless, her attitude that "she wanted [her affair] seen. She wanted it validated in the wild,"[7] gives the story an authentic ring, as does her sentiment that "the worst part was making sure the red-haired doctor was suffering as much as she was. She wanted him miserable."[8] That is not a particularly noble sentiment but, again, an honest one.

The third section of the story is told from the doctor's point of view, set off by a white space, which keeps the transition from jarring the reader. In fact, it is a crucial part of the story—crucial that the doctor's perspective on all this is aired, because from *his* consciousness emerges the true crux of the story. "Where was the will in all of this? The married man wondered . . . . Who was she, after all? he wondered. This woman who was doing this to him."[9]

The story then reverts to Anna's side of things. She is greatly frustrated with the affair and vows to go back to North Carolina—where she is found, of course, at the story's beginning. And now that she is back home she begins composing the stories she had promised her editor, taking solace in the certainty that her work is how she defines herself.

Contrarily, Gilchrist's understanding of the Anna Hand character falters grievously in the novel *The Anna Papers* and in the novella "Winter," the first in the trio of Hand-related novellas gathered in *I Cannot Get You Close Enough*. This novel and this novella are bleak, humorless portraits of Anna Hand as a continual busybody, discontent with her own life and feeling the need to turn to running the lives of her family members. The two works are close-fitting companions, the novella picking up exactly where the novel left off; but the novella is hardly free-standing, since a full, meaningful understanding of it is predicated on prior familiarity with the novel.

The Anna Papers opens with a "Preamble," which delivers a face slap: Anna's suicide. Then flashing back a couple years, Anna is in New York City and her best friend has just died after a long illness. In a prophetic statement, Anna insists to another friend that *she* will never die in a hospital. But both she and her baby-doctor lover—reappearing from the story "Anna, Part I"— have the impression that something is physically wrong with her; but Anna hasn't time for a checkup, for she's moving back to North Carolina, where "Anna, Part I" had left her. But she continues to maintain her affair with the doctor in New York City, even though now it is on a long-distance basis. Soon she decides to abandon her house in the North Carolina mountains and live among her family in Charlotte, presumably answering some tribal or even animalistic call to return to her birthplace—as if her sense of physical unease has sharpened within her a receptivity to the pull of her "ancestral" homeland.

Anna has had husbands, but never a child; and now she embarks on a "project" that she rationalizes as compensation for that absence in her life. But at the same time, she insists to herself and others that this project is a necessary action for the good of the family. Unfortunately, it is a *dishonest* project, an unconvincing one that makes the novel unconvincing, and thus it implodes in upon itself.

Anna has learned that her brother Daniel had fathered a child by his now deceased first wife, a Native American from Oklahoma—a fact even Daniel was not aware of until this daughter contacted the famous writer Anna Hand. Over Daniel's objections, Anna takes it upon herself to go bring the now teenage girl, Olivia, to North Carolina, to the bosom of the Hand family. The thing is, Daniel already has a teenage daughter there with him in Charlotte—Jessie, his daughter by his second wife, who is now off living an eccentric life in England.

Anna has moments of clarity as to her true motives in this business with her long-lost niece, referring to herself, *to* herself, as "Little Mother Superior, imposing my will on them [her family] as usual."[10] But such flashes of self-realization do not deter her from her cause; and, unfortunately, her brief occasions of clarity in terms of what she is doing and why are not indications of actual *strength* of character and insight, but of selfishness and need to control other peoples' lives as a way of getting to the bottom of her own issues.

Anna Hand had great appeal in the two short stories that first introduced her: an intriguing character who promised that getting to know her better would be pleasure. In the Anna novel, however, what good is seen in her? What goodness is there, really, to counter her bald need to control? And this obsession of hers with "rescuing" her niece is unconvincing to a disastrous degree: disastrous because so much of the novel's pages are consumed with this exercise of Anna's that is given no real legitimacy in readers' eyes. The fundamental problem, then, with the character of Anna *and* this novel is that the reader simply is not made to believe that this is such a huge issue for Anna.

Compensation for not having a child of her own? She has plenty of nieces and nephews to love, particularly Daniel's other daughter, Jessie. Yes, indeed, it is true, Olivia contacted Anna first of all her Hand relatives; it was by this initial contact that the family and even Daniel, her father, was made aware of Olivia's existence. That Anna took it so compulsively, so selfishly, so self-importantly, is what cannot be believed or sympathized with. Do-gooders are fine if they are seen with feet of clay and they come dressed in irony; but the issue here is not whether Anna has feet of clay, but that we simply do not comprehend why she is doing "good" in this instance when the impression of her so far in the novel is certainly not one of a generous person.

This situation is deadly for the novel's sake. Readers will feel themselves drumming their fingers out of impatience—even out of anger—over Gilchrist's insistence this lost niece issue become such a large part of Anna's life. A famous writer who left a lover behind in New York to come home and write a new book, and at the same time has a growing sense of ill health and mortality—this person would be involved so heavily in such a piece of business that is not *really* her business? Why? This simply is *not* Anna's story—it is Daniel's story, and it is Olivia's story. Anna should be at the periphery of it, not at the center of it—not the *cause* of it. It is a trumped up circumstance in terms of Anna's participation in it. Having been contacted by Olivia, Anna, in a more honest and believable act than the one Gilchrist contrived for her, would more naturally turn the problem over to Daniel and perhaps help him with it, but not dominate and dictate it. So we are being led to believe that rescuing Olivia is a primary concern for a person—Anna—who has turned away from her family to follow a path to personal freedom but now decides to toss the family net over the head of someone she doesn't know, all in the name of providing material benefit and advantages to this unknown entity? Why? Even seeing it in the light of Anna's experiencing guilt over having neglected her family for so long that she overdoes this situation in an attempt to assuage her guilt—even then it still rings false as a consuming issue for Anna. Even if Anna is hearing a distant, still-faint call of mortality, why—we simply *don't* know—is this the issue she must tackle with such passion? Gilchrist has no answer to that question, and without one Anna cannot be accepted on the terms Gilchrist has given.

But let *us* not get as consumed as Anna does with the "rescuing" of Olivia, for other things do go on in *The Anna Papers* besides that story line. Anna is still very much involved with her boyfriend, the red haired baby doctor back in New York. Typical for affairs, this one troubles its participants. At one point, the doctor exclaims, "Shit. What in the name of God did we do this to each other for?"[11] But later in a self-contradiction that is natural to a situation like this, he asserts, "We deserve our passions."[12] Witness this succinct, very realistic exchange between the two of them:

She raised her eyes. "I changed my mind [about seeing him again]. I will be your mistress, or whatever you will have me for. This is okay. Some love, some grief. I love you."

"I love you back. When will you be coming to New York?"

"This summer. As soon as I finish this book."

"I'll see you then. Call me when you know what day."[13]

Gilchrist's ear for dialogue is pristine. (And, tangentially, this piece of conversation suggests that a novel about Anna Hand would have been more successful had it been all about her relationship with the doctor.)

In addition to bringing her niece Olivia from Oklahoma to be with the rest of the family in North Carolina, and besides her continued relationship with the married doctor in New York, another issue is at play in Anna's life: her growing awareness of something wrong in the functioning of her body. With that in mind, she asks one of her sisters, Helen, to be her literary executor, along with a poet friend of Anna's in Boston. Anna is eventually diagnosed with cancer, and she decides to take matters finally into her own hands by killing herself, because "the alternative was a bed in a hospital and knives and terror. One big terror or a lot of little terrors. Death was going to win, either way."[14]

By this act, which occurs about two-thirds of the way through the novel, the main character disappears from its pages; and even though Anna continues to cast a shadow over the rest of the narrative, her disappearance—or, more particularly, her replacement as the main character by her sister, Helen, whom we have only *briefly* met thus far in the novel—simply flies in the reader's face as a flaw of execution and compromises the effect of what was presumably Gilchrist's overall intention: to limn the after-effects of someone's life and death on loved ones left behind. We simply don't *feel* the poignancy and power like Gilchrist must want us to; and we don't feel it because we lack both sympathy for, and understanding of, Anna's motives. Yes, indeed, it can be granted that Anna was a large enough figure to cast a shadow over family and friends after her death, but she never seemed deeper than a shadow to *readers* even when she was alive. We have already discussed how her obsession with her niece seemed contrived, but it must also be admitted that her relationship with her New York lover screams for more development, and her suicide is unconvincing. It is unbelievable that she would give up the fight that easily; if it is to be believed that she would take on a big problem like more or less kidnapping her niece in the face of her brother's adversity, then it cannot be believed that Anna would give in to her illness so quickly and easily, to say nothing of how melodramatically the act comes across. And now, upon her demise, her story becomes Helen's story— which is probably what the novel should have been about in the first place: stay-at-home Helen's reactions to her famous sister's return to their home- town and then to her sister's illness and death.

This last third of the novel makes a *better* novel. What Helen learns of the personal side of Anna's life by going through and organizing all of Anna's papers—as she was charged to do by Anna's appointment of her as literary executor—turns out to be a more provocative and certainly more interesting way to fashion a portrait of Anna: by "second-Hand," as it were. Helen is a character who is more clearly drawn and more attractive as a person than Anna, and her perspective on her famous sister achieves greater dimension and even subtlety than the straight telling of Anna's story from her own view. It works better this way because Helen *is* telling *her* own story: her reactions to her famous sister, that is. She is not taking over someone else's life and pre- tending it is really about her, as Anna does—or, more appropriately, as Gilchrist *did* for Anna. Helen leaves her boring husband and problem chil- dren and staid existence, and she goes to Boston to live with the coexecutor of Anna's estate, the magnetic poet John Carmichael; and how much more engaging is *that* story than Anna's obsession with her niece.

The first novella in the collection of three novellas *I Cannot Get You Close Enough* brings renewed disappointment. (As indicated earlier in this chapter, I am passing over the actual *next* book after *The Anna Papers* for the time being, because the novella collection *I Cannot Get You Close Enough* takes up the story of the Hand family where *The Anna Papers* left off.) "Winter" is the title of the first novella, and it is in the form of a manuscript Anna left behind after her suicide: one of the papers, presumably, that her sister Helen had to organize as Anna's executor. In time sequence, though, it is a flashback to events *prior* to those taking place in *The Anna Papers*; and it is with a sinking heart that one realizes it is about Anna's obsession with *another* niece, Jessie, her brother Daniel's other daughter—by his second wife—from whom he wrestled custody, therefore raising Jessie in the bosom of the Hand family in Charlotte. The second paragraph of the novella opens with the dark words "If I am going to save Jessie. . . ."[15]

Anna is off to rescue another niece, but why? Specifically, "Winter" deals with Anna's investigation into her former sister-in-law Sheila's disreputable life to gather evidence against her for an upcoming custody trial over Jessie. In reference to her own family, the Hands, and in somewhat of a defense of her actions here in this particular episode, Anna admits, "power is all any of us know."[16]

Again, as in *The Anna Papers*, that is a feeble defense, not going nearly far enough to explain Anna's actions, not sufficiently excusing her for her almost ruthless involvement in other people's business. It bears repeating, as in *The Anna Papers*, that these events in "Winter" vis à vis her nieces are not *her* stories, but the stories of her nieces and her brother, and consequently Anna's place in the center, her dominance as primary character, is manufactured. As is true in *The Anna Papers*, making Anna's participation in these events tenable, to make them real and acceptable, she should have been given the role of supporter, not savior; as Gilchrist has it, her controlling streak is offensive in this context, and it should have been directed into another "project" that really is *her* issue and about *her* life.

Other usual qualities of Gilchrist's fiction suffer in the novel and the novella accordingly. Her voice lacks vibrancy; her dialogue is contrived (with notable exceptions being the exchanges between Anna and her doctor boyfriend, which, as we have suggested, offer further indication of another direction the novel might have taken and thus been more successful). The humor Gilchrist usually weaves into her narratives is missing in these two pieces—as if it were necessary to expunge it here to prove the seriousness of all this niece business. Further, as the atmospheres of New Orleans and Fayetteville are felt through all the senses in her previous fiction set in those two places, from the Anna novel and this first Anna novella absolutely *no* sense of the textures and tone of Charlotte, North Carolina comes across—as void of atmosphere as if Gilchrist has never visited the city for herself.

But dawn breaks over the Anna Hand sequence to usher in a welcome sunrise, in the second novella appearing in *I Cannot Get You Close Enough*, which is called "DeHavilland Hand." Finally, the story of Anna's niece Olivia is told *correctly*: told as *Olivia's* story, not as Anna's. The first line cogently establishes the narrative's intent and framework: "The creation and first sixteen years of life of Olivia de Havilland Hand . . . ."[17]

Daniel Hand, it will be remembered, is Anna's brother—one of her brothers, actually. This novella casts backstory light on his early marriage to Summer, a Native American from Oklahoma. Daniel, not a good student, "liked to do life, not read about it."[18] This being the late 1960s, where better for a young person to experience life than the Bay area in California? For her part, Summer "had become bored with her brothers and sisters and trying to be a Cherokee Indian in the modern world."[19] She, too, headed to Berkeley.

Daniel and Summer marry soon after meeting, and shortly after that they go to visit his family back in Charlotte: a disastrous experience, for the Hands do not accept her; and in 10 days' time she flees back to Oklahoma—pregnant, but her condition unbeknown to Daniel, who has the marriage annulled.

Summer dies in childbirth; her sister raises Summer's daughter, Olivia. By this time—the story's actual present time—Olivia is 12 years old and asking about her father, and anticipating his advent into her life any time now. By an odd, awfully coincidental circumstance, an English teacher of Olivia's uses in her classroom an anthology that contains a story by someone who Olivia will learn is her aunt, the famous writer Anna Hand. The rest of the novella, then, concerns Olivia's problematic life in North Carolina once she has not only contacted Anna Hand, but also gone to live with, and been absorbed into, the Hand clan. "I guess," Olivia ponders when reflecting on her old, wild habits, "that's my childhood I have to leave behind."[20]

This is a situation the reader can relate to; a teenager leaves home and family behind, to go live in another state with the other side of her family. It is a poignant situation, a realistic one. But an element of strain still exists in the telling of it, as if Gilchrist has some distance to go to discover the most direct, resonant, reader-inclusive approach to explaining the effect of Anna Hand on the members of her extensive family, particularly on her two nieces, the two daughters of her brother Daniel.

Gilchrist solves all these problems in the third of the three novellas, "A Summer in Maine," in which she finds the perfect path by which to relate the concept of how much Anna Hand imprinted her family members. The setting is a big, rambling summer home on the coast of Maine. Gilchrist corrals several of her recurrent—and in most instances interrelated—characters, each of whom alternates in narrating events from his or her perspective as the long summer progresses. The first narrator up to bat is inarguably Gilchrist's best narrator on any occasion: Traceleen, the black maid who works for Crystal Manning of New Orleans. Traceleen was first encountered in a four-story sequence in the collection *Victory over Japan*, and that quartet remains in the mind as some of the most effective of all of Gilchrist's stories. To meet Traceleen again here, to hear her eloquent voice once more, and enjoy her views on life, grounded in her unique homespun wisdom, is indeed a pleasure. The mosaic effect employed here—the alternating sharing of and commentary on events by a wide circle of characters, their testimonies a few pages or several pages in length, as they go around the table again and again—is not only an efficient but also an imaginative way to observe the various effects of Anna Hand's recent death on the people who knew her the longest, her family.

The house in Maine that they all go to visit is owned by a reclusive old lady, a friend of Crystal's in New Orleans, who was, in her day, a famous actress. Her name is Noel, and she had just received a letter from Anna's sister Helen, asking to see the correspondence Anna had sent her over the years, Anna and Noel having been friends for a long time. Helen, it will be remembered, is Anna's literary executor and thus in charge of getting Anna's papers all together. Noel is determined that Helen won't get her hands on these letters, and the main reason she wants Crystal to stay in her summer house in Maine is so she will take their mutual friend, the painter Lydia, along with her; and Noel can trust Lydia to secure the letters and bring them to her.

Crystal invites more people than just Lydia to join the summer party, including Traceleen and Traceleen's niece, but also King, Crystal's son by her first marriage, her cousin Daniel Hand (the late Anna's brother), and Daniel's two daughters, Jessie and Olivia, Anna's dual obsessions, it will be remembered.

Despite a large cast of characters, each character is rendered with careful shading. Gilchrist's supple raconteur's voice—"All night, every night all summer, while we were sleeping, the ocean was tugging on us, calling us back to our senses"[21]—is laced with humor. "That's the mating dance. In the mating dance the men talk and the women listen. Later only the women talk."[22] But it is also tinged with violence and loaded with sexuality. Her dialogue has perfect pitch. And, most importantly, all her characterizations here ring with honesty; as each character contributes his or her series of short monologues, they tell their side of the summer in Maine exactly as each *should* tell it. In other words, no one is telling a story he or she really doesn't own.

The summer proceeds with all variations of domestic drama springing up and snapping like lightning, all of which climaxes with Anna's niece Jessie and Crystal's teenage son, King, having to get married because Jessie is pregnant. So, another generation of the Hand family is in the making; and the story of Anna and her nieces can now be walked away from with full, comfortable appreciation of the resonance of Anna, not only with her siblings, but undoubtedly also over generations after that.

In conclusion, the best piece of writing about Anna herself is the short story "Anna: Part I" from *Drunk with Love*. It is Anna's story, not someone else's story; it concerns real and important issues in Anna's life, not overblown secondary ones like what is found in *The Anna Papers* and the novella "Winter" in *I Cannot Get You Close Enough*.

Anna Vaux summarized *The Anna Papers* in her article entitled "Spoilt Southerners," which appeared in the *Times Literary Supplement*, in this cogent way: "It was a fragmentary book, without much plot, which dealt mainly with the story of her two nieces . . . and petered out in a dispiriting trail of oddments and posthumous papers." And she goes on to comment on the novella collection *I Cannot Get You Close Enough*, "It's not so much 'another saga,' as the publishers announce, as the old one revisited . . . there is no shape or design or ironic distance."[23]

Chapter 6

More Visits with Recurrent Characters (*Light Can Be Both Wave and Particle*)

GILCHRIST'S NEXT BOOK—actually, the book that in terms of publishing chronology came between the novel *The Anna Papers* and the trio of Anna Hand–related novellas *I Cannot Get You Close Enough*—is another strong collection of short stories called *Light Can Be Both Wave and Particle,* published in 1989. The stories are arranged by "category:" three stories featuring Rhoda Manning; a three-story Nora Jane Whittington sequence; then another trio of stories, the first of which is unconnected to any previous Gilchrist character, but the second and third ones being sequels to her first novel, *The Annunciation*; and the final two stories bring us back to very familiar Gilchrist territory: a Traceleen story, in which this sharp-eyed witness shares the latest goings on of her boss, Rhoda's cousin Crystal Manning of New Orleans, and another Rhoda appearance, this time in a novella.

Two of the stories rise above the others; all are good, but these two in particular soar. In fact, one of these two easily can be considered Gilchrist's masterpiece in the short story form. A Rhoda story, it is titled "Some Blue Hills at Sundown," and its length is a mere five pages. But "mere" is relative, for regardless of this *short* story's brevity, or *because* of it—because it is such a cogent limning of character—it ranks as the best Rhoda story so far. Not only does Gilchrist distill the essence of the teenage Rhoda in pure, concentrated form, like producing a strong, savory, not the least bitter liqueur, but also, in such amazingly brief space, she imparts to Rhoda an admirable strength going well beyond the sheer stubbornness that, up to this point, has been our experience with Rhoda and has seemed to be the basis—the *substance*, rather—of her fortitude. Certainly, unmistakable stubbornness runs through her veins in this lovely story; she is not free of it, by any means. It remains a major component of Rhoda Manning's constitution, after all. The situation here is simply that Rhoda's persistence in trying to get what she wants is not annoying, which it has been on several previous occasions, but is instead something by which an understanding of and sympathy toward her are extended. In this story Rhoda is able to stand above her adolescent self-centeredness and take an important step toward a mature acceptance of the way the world works, even if its workings are not always congruous with the way she would prefer them to happen.

The first paragraph demonstrates Gilchrist's appreciation that the best way to open a story is by thrusting the reader, with hat still on head, as it were, quickly and directly into it. In an excellent display of exacting maximum effect from minimal words, the first sentence establishes the story's whole frame: "It was the last time Rhoda would ever see Bob Rosen in her life." The whole first paragraph rounds out the situation with great skill: "Perhaps she knew that the whole time she was driving to meet him, the long drive through the November fields, down the long narrow state of Kentucky, driving due west, then across the Ohio River and up into the flat-topped hills of Southern Illinois."[1]

Rhoda lives now in Kentucky, then; until quite recently she lived in southern Illinois (where, along with southern Indiana, the series of previously discussed Rhoda-as-child stories have been set). The second paragraph reveals her purpose in making this journey back up to the north: to see her boyfriend whom she had to leave behind when she and her family moved away, and he is just out of the hospital, having had another operation. They have not seen each other in two months. Rhoda's eagerness to see him is palpable: "If it had been any other time in her life or any other boyfriend she would have been stopping every fifty miles to look at herself in the mirror or spray her wrists with perfume or smooth the wrinkles from her skirt. As it was, she drove steadily up into the hills, the lengthy shadows all around her."[2]

Rhoda's mother had not wanted her to make the trip, so her father, more to spite his wife (since their marriage is "half-broken" and laden with "tears and sadness")[3] than acting out of any great consideration for his daughter, lets her use his Cadillac, "six thousand dollars' worth of brand-new car, a fortune of a car in nineteen fifty-three."[4] (This piece of information quickly establishes the time period here.)

When Rhoda arrives at her destination, we see the essence of Bob's appearance and how his energy is being consumed by his illness: "One foot on top of the other foot, his soft gray trousers loose around the ankles, his soft white skin, his tall lanky body fighting every minute for life."

In two beautiful lines, Gilchrist makes unequivocal the significance of Rhoda's trip to visit the young man she hadn't seen in several weeks: "It was the first time in two months that she had been happy. Now, suddenly, it seemed as if this moment would be enough to last forever, would make up for all the time that would follow."[5] (The last few words seem to be a portent, given Bob's illness.) After a brief conversation, Rhoda lobs a proposition to him, couched in her own teenage way of expression: "I want to do it."[6] She goes on to indicate her belief that Bob had promised this would happen.

With a cockiness that doesn't so much *mask* a sensitivity as work in tandem with it, Bob answers Rhoda's request by not exactly brushing her off but by simply emphasizing the reality of the situation: its illegality. But the truth of his feelings for Rhoda, behind the words he has spoken to her, becomes clear when he pulls her to him and kisses her again; and in reference to her desire for them to make love, he admits that he wants to, even if he can't.

Only three pages into the story at this point and a clear reason why Rhoda has arrived here to visit her boyfriend has been defined. Also readily given is an appreciation of Rhoda's headstrong and determined personality (a thorough enough appreciation for it to amount to respect, which is, of course, certainly not the case with other stories about Rhoda leaving childhood and standing on the verge of her teenage years), a solid perception of the parental conditions she left behind, and an enjoyment of the sweetness and maturity of the college-age boy she came here to visit. All of this without pages of elaboration and history being spelled out; but neither without a sense of being short-changed in terms of the necessary information for a satisfying, meaningful reaction to the characters and events.

Rhoda presses her "suit" with Bob one more time, insisting that this night will be their only chance *ever*. Again the wise-beyond-his-years Bob gently sidetracks her, and it now occurs to Rhoda that she was "like a pet dog to him. . . just some little kid he's nice to."[7]

But, then, in a few immaculate, flint-tough, and even haunting lines, Gilchrist delivers the crux of the story: "Rhoda shuddered. It was so exciting. . . . This is really happening, she was thinking. This feeling, this loving him more than anything in the world and in a second it will be over. It ends as it happens and it will never be again in any way, never happen again or stop happening."[8]

Rhoda not only has divined, in a flash, the reality of her predicament with Bob but also has grown up a significant degree. The story's conclusion is stunning in its sheerness, completed in two sentences: "He was counting the months he might live. He thought it would be twenty-four but it turned out to be a lifetime after all."[9] Admittedly, those last two lines are another example of Gilchrist' too abrupt point of view shifts—in this case, of course, from Rhoda's suddenly to Bob's. But this time, no exception has to be taken to it; this time an exception can be *made* for it for the simple reason that this information renders the story poignant rather than tragic. (Of course not every critic is going to be impressed by the same work; for instance, in responding to this story, Dorie LaRue maintains that in it "Rhoda [is] playing Scarlett O'Hara to a fault. The rebelliousness gimmick here is wrung for all it is worth.")[10]

The other most outstanding story in this collection, while not the masterpiece that is "Some Blue Hills at Sundown," is "Traceleen Turns East"; and as the title indicates, it features that wonderful storyteller Traceleen, maid to Crystal Manning, Rhoda's cousin, who lives in comfort in New Orleans. Traceleen, it will be remembered from previous encounters, does not talk about herself much, preferring instead to play the role of narrator, and to recount the latest goings-on in her boss's up-and-down and always exciting life. Traceleen's style of telling a story, not focusing on herself and slipping in plenty of aside comments—almost little pieces of editorialization—gives her plenty of time and room to share her keen judgment, balanced perspective, and innate wisdom. These are the hallmarks of this self-effacing but strong and absolutely lovable woman.

It seems that Crystal has given up dieting and exercise, according to Traceleen having "lost heart and stopped caring."[11] Traceleen is puzzled by Crystal's giving up; but the wise and perceptive Traceleen quickly comes to understand the reasons: first, it becomes increasingly difficult to lose weight the older one gets, and second, Crystal's dieting caused dental problems. So, she and Traceleen—ever-devoted Traceleen—enroll in a yoga class. Traceleen had been reluctant at first, but her pastor convinced her that "some heathen practices"[12] would broaden her horizons.

Four months of yoga do indeed get Crystal's weight and Traceleen's blood pressure under control, and Crystal's recovery from oral surgery, to repair the damage done by her excessive dieting, is speedier because of it. But there is something else, another benefit from their weeks of practicing yoga: their growing strength, their path to becoming samurai. And their increased mental and physical power get put to good use when one afternoon an armed robber invades their unlocked house and holds them hostage. Later, after the frightening episode is safely resolved, their yoga teacher indicated that Traceleen "became a samurai when [she] had the brainstorm to fake a heart attack"[13]—which is how the home invasion and hostage taking were brought to a head, and unhappily so for the gun-toting robber.

Not surprisingly Crystal and Traceleen continue their yoga, for, after all, they must keep up their strength. This story is sheer amusement, a colorful snapshot of contemporary life and habits as viewed from the I'm-part-of-it-but-also-*not*-part-of-it Traceleen, keeping one foot in Crystal's plights and the other foot outside them—to maintain her composure, if not her sanity.

In addition to the Rhoda story "Some Blue Hills at Sundown," there are three more in the collection in which she features. "The Tree Fort" and "The Time Capsule" are both set in southern Indiana during World War II, a time and place in which Rhoda has been visited several times before, where Rhoda spent significant years of her childhood. These two companion stories lend further support to the idea that the stories of Rhoda as a little girl tend to be among the strongest Rhoda stories because of the good understanding they give of the inner workings of a girl's mind as she struggles for self-assertion and self-identity in a family crowded with a domineering father and a young knight-in-shining-armor-in-the-making older brother.

The fourth and last Rhoda piece in this collection is the novella length "Mexico," at 70 pages the longest single "visitation" with Rhoda thus far. At this point in time, she, at age fifty-three, "has run out of men. That's how the trip to Mexico began. It began because Rhoda was bored."[14] In what may strike readers as Gilchrist's own version of Hemingway's novel *The Sun Also Rises*, Rhoda's brother Dudley invites Rhoda to go with him and their (male) cousin to Mexico, to investigate some great bird-hunting territory. The three of them rendezvous in San Antonio and drive down below the border, Rhoda's thoughts, as they drive, centered on the toughness of the ties of family, from whom she derives not only necessary diversion right now in her bored state but also sustenance and solace in her husbandless and even boyfriendless state; in other words, her brother and male cousin currently fulfill her need for constant male company and attention.

In Mexico Rhoda meets Dudley's Mexican girlfriend, and they all go to a bullfight; Rhoda is immediately intoxicated—by a matador they observe, that is. Dudley and their cousin are dead-set against her carrying out her intention of having a quick liaison with him. Later in the trip, she falls and damages her ankle, and she returns home to a relatively stationary life for the time being—her ankle in a cast and she in a wheelchair. The trip to Mexico certainly had its downsides—besides her injury, she never managed to hook up with the sexy bullfighter. But the adventure did reinforce in Rhoda the strength of family connections.

The problem with this long story is that the adult Rhoda, as experienced here, seems little different from Anna Hand in *The Anna Papers* and Amanda McCamey in *The Annunciation*. They are basically cut from the same cloth; they are fundamentally one and the same character—strong, headstrong, but always in need of a man to ensure complete stabilization in life. Intelligent, articulate, a writer, or involved in academia in some fashion. Stubborn to a fault, certain of their "better-than-ness," and if not sure of their correctness every time in making decisions about their own lives, at least definitely sure in deciding how other people should lead their lives. Confident and self-centered. At least Amanda and Rhoda are not as controlling as Anna Hand—at least this is a difference among the three of them.

It is as if in longer pieces, at least in the novels and novellas examined so far, Gilchrist often loses her ability to individualize her female characters; in her short stories she isolates a thread or two or three of their essence and personality, and in the smaller picture, ironically, these few threads stand out and give the character a distinctiveness. To carry the metaphor farther, then: When Gilchrist weaves large tapestries, the individualizing threads are lost in the weave of the big picture, and consequently the tapestries emerge rather indistinct from one another.

Further evidence of Gilchrist's greater practice of character delineation—of character *individualization*—in the short story form is offered in this collection in a sequence of stories featuring the recurrent character Nora Jane Whittington. In fact more reasons are given here to call Nora Jane, along with the child-Rhoda, Gilchrist's most compelling, interesting, appealing, and best drawn of her recurrent characters. Actually, of three stories of the Nora Jane suite, only the first, "The Starlight Express," features her as the main character; the other two stories, "Light Can Be Both Wave and Particle" and "First Harmonics," are tight-fitting companion pieces that focus on, in the former, a character who is acquainted in an unusual way with Nora Jane and, in the latter one, a character *in*directly connected to her: *two* degrees of separation, in this case.

"The Starlight Express" takes up where Nora Jane was left last: in the story "Drunk with Love," in the collection of the same name. Nora Jane is seven months pregnant with twins, living again with her boyfriend Sandy, whom she came to California to join, following him there from New Orleans. But, as the story opens, Sandy—true to this noncommittal nature—has just fled, leaving the very pregnant Nora Jane at the house they were living in together on a beach somewhere south of San Francisco. The point of view alternates between Nora Jane, her other California boyfriend Freddy Harwood, and a young Chinese geneticist named Lin Tan Sing, who did the lab work on Nora Jane's amniocentesis, and whom we met briefly in "Drunk with Love." But as Gilchrist has shown herself capable of in some other stories, these point of view shifts are not overly abrupt, not too jarring. In this instance they strengthen the story. To make that point further, Freddy Harwood is Gilchrist's most interesting, most endearing male character, and his perspective on Nora Jane is both entertaining and illuminating.

The Chinese geneticist Lin Tan is embarking on a vacation, and he boards the same train as Nora Jane, the Starlight Express, as she seeks a good place to live, now that Sandy has abandoned her—namely, with Freddy in his house in the remote northern part of the state. Nora Jane has informed Freddy in advance of her impending arrival, and he has mixed feelings about getting reinvolved with her, reminding himself that her babies aren't his; but, on the other side of this coin, "Why do I want her at all? Because I like to talk to her, that's why."[15]

Meanwhile, Nora Jane and Lin Tan fall into conversation on the train; and two and two are put together and they arrive at the realization it was Lin Tan who conducted the lab work on Nora Jane's amnio. Lin Tan tells her that he cast *I Ching* for her daughters, seeing "great honors for them and gifts of music brought to the world."[16]

The train soon arrives at Nora Jane's destination, and she and her new friend part. Freddy is waiting for her; and despite Nora Jane's insistence to him that she doesn't really know what she's doing, that she is pretty much just winging it, it is to Gilchrist's credit that Nora Jane is such a well-conceived, well-developed, and well-presented character that *the reader* knows that Nora Jane can be counted on to do the right thing in the end. That Nora Jane is set up so sympathetically is the reason why the reader's opinion can be nothing but supportive of her coming to be with Freddy, that such as act is exactly what she should be doing in her condition—the wise thing for her babies, the health of which should be, and is, her chief concern.

But when the babies come, Nora Jane is in grave physical distress and needs to be rescued from Freddy's remote house by helicopter. At story's end, though, all is good: mother and twin girls are fine. The one called Lydia is crying, telling herself that she is "laying my first guilt trip on my people."[17]

The next story, "Light Can Be Both Wave and Particle," picks up the previous story's initial storyline: that which concerned geneticist Lin Tan, who now arrives in Washington State carrying pleasant thoughts of his encounter with Nora Jane on the train; but now Lin Tan meets another young woman, Margaret McElvoy of Fayetteville, Arkansas. He is smitten, and she is taken with him, too. "A queen is inside of this girl,"[18] Lin Tan thinks. Their instant, mutual feelings for each other compels Gilchrist to tip-top story-telling eloquence, as when she says, about Lin Tan, "He laughed a great hearty laugh, a laugh he had forgotten he possessed. It was the best laugh he had ever laughed in the United States."[19] Margaret takes him home to Fayetteville to meet her parents. Her father is a poet and teacher at the university there, and Lin Tan impresses him. To himself, the father says, in praise of not only himself but his daughter's good sense in picking a mate, "Goddammit, I raised a girl with a brain in her head, hitting on all cylinders the morning she plucked this one from the sea."[20] Margaret and Lin Tan become engaged while they are visiting her parents.

The next story, "First Harmonics," which is the third and last piece in this warm series of interlocking Nora Jane stories, is just a brief sketch, but nevertheless it achieves a sheerness of poignancy; and despite its brevity, it is completely discrete and capable of standing on its own as well as fitting in tightly with the other two stories in the triptych. The story concerns Lin Tan's boyhood friend from China, Randal Yung, who, a scientist here in the U.S., has suddenly become famous for being the first to capture and kill an atom in a laboratory. Randal is "sick" of the whole thing: of his fame, of his photograph appearing everywhere in the press, of the rumors and distortions that get written about him.

He gets a letter from his parents back in China informing him that his two goldfish died, which saddens him. "Larger and larger the fish had grown. Then Randal had left and gone to California. Now the fish were dead."[21] That is the end of the story, as simple as that; but it is to be read as a fable about the direct relation between cause and effect in the balance of the universe.

The three remaining stories in the collection are interesting but certainly minor pieces. "The Man Who Kicked Cancer's Ass" is further evidence that Gilchrist can indeed create a viable male character. "The Song of Songs" and "Life on the Earth" are both sequels to her first novel, *The Annunciation*, and reveal that the young father of Amanda's new baby survived the car crash that ended that novel; but for the reader who has not read the novel, these stories unfortunately signify little.

A review in *Quill & Quire* was generally unfavorable about the collection as a whole, proffering this observation: "Peopled by characters who frequently verge on stereotype and driven forward by plotting that often telegraphs its intentions well in advance, these narrative seldom rise about the comfortably conventional."[22] And a review in *Publisher's Weekly* called into question the use of recurrent characters by maintaining "too many of them [the stories in this collection] seems self-indulgent and self-referential, as though Gilchrist is writing only for readers familiar with her established characters."[23]

Chapter 7

Two Hits and a Miss (*Net of Jewels, Starcarbon, Anabasis*)

GILCHRIST'S THIRD NOVEL, *Net of Jewels*, which was published in 1992, postpones premature conclusions concerning her superior ability in the short story form over the novel, for this novel is read with absolute joy and admiration. *Net of Jewels* is a jewel. It is unique in Gilchrist's oeuvre: in that it is a *novel* about Rhoda Manning, not stories or a novella. With its appearance, Gilchrist asserts her having overcome previous problems with the form. This is a novel totally secure in character development, unquestionably solid in structure, and, particularly important after the experience of *The Anna Papers,* demonstrating the author's complete mastery of material: all issues and problems and concerns and activities that have been assigned to Rhoda are definitely *hers* in which to be involved.

Net of Jewels is a first-person narrative: a deeply absorbing, personal recounting of Rhoda's life from the end of her freshman year in college to her mid-twenties, at which point she is the mother of two little boys, and her early-made marriage is in collapse. Its exceptional qualities demand attention before discussing the plot itself. As she has done effectively in her short stories, Gilchrist plunges the reader directly into the action, which she did not do in her first two novels. While not as crucial a technique in the novel as in the short story—given the spaciousness the novel can claim—diving into the story spares the author the fancy but often fatal footwork it takes an author to rescue readers from a slow start and convince them to continue reading. In this third novel, Gilchrist has applied lessons from her own short story writing experience and permits the reader the enjoyment of diving in.

The second salient characteristic of this novel is not an issue of technique but one of conception and presentation: specifically, how Gilchrist conceives and presents one of her most famous and recurrent female characters, Rhoda Manning. Simply put, Rhoda is likeable here, as well as understandable; whereas in some previous Rhoda stories, particularly those featuring her as a young woman, she had been downright unlikable and spoiled, her selfishness, self-centeredness, and headstrongness not tempered by softer, more approachable traits. But in this novel that problem does not exist; it has been fixed by the expansiveness of the form, for Gilchrist takes full advantage of the length more or less prescribed by the definition of the "novel" to carefully build the character of Rhoda and, in the process, to make certain that the darker sides of her personality are understandable, or at least recognizable for their provenance, and the reader thus can weigh them fairly against the totality of her persona. In a word, *sympathetic*. Gilchrist makes Rhoda sympathetic here.

It is an interesting situation that, in the stories focusing on Rhoda as a girl, she comes across as likable and, while precocious and boasting a very distinctive personality even at her young age, understandable as typical *for* her age. That is what makes the Rhoda-as-child stories so charming: she is obviously a smart little girl, but at the same time she is *still* a little girl, with childish issues and a child's perspective on the world. But in the stories thus far about Rhoda as a young married woman, she grates—irritating in her self-absorption.

The most obvious evidence of this situation is in the embedding into this novel about Rhoda of the short story "1957, A Romance," which appeared in Gilchrist's first short story collection, *In the Land of Dreamy Dreams,* which was discussed in a previous chapter. It will be remembered in that story that Rhoda is separated from her husband and back home living with her parents in Alabama, with her two little boys; and she has her father fly with her to Houston for an abortion, after which she celebrates the maintenance of her youthful figure. Rhoda is at her selfish, manipulative worst in that story, leaving a bad taste. But when the story is set like a piece of a puzzle into the larger narrative of the novel, it is not so much that its sour taste is diluted by the many, many other events and episodes in the novel as it is a case of when seeing *this* particular episode, a very unhappy one, in the context of where Rhoda's life had taken her up to this point and where it will go after this important decision of Rhoda's, we understand *it* and *her* and do not experience the same reaction at all. Reading that story as an episode in the novel, the reader agrees that that is exactly what Rhoda would do, having married this young man for all the wrong reasons, and because she has had previous difficult childbirths. Yes, life is all about Rhoda, but at least in the novel, how she developed that attitude and the price she had to pay for it are seen and understood. Again, in a word, *sympathy*. Sympathy was a very important element missing in the story "1957: A Romance" *as* a short story.

Now, let's see just what the novel is about. It concerns Rhoda in young womanhood and the two poles of her life at that point—the two opposing gravitational poles *on* her life—both of which are men. One pole, the first one, the first to establish its unavoidable presence, is her father: "My daddy is a vain and beautiful man who thinks of his children as extensions of his personality. Our entire lives were supposed to be lights to shine upon his stage. . . . You have to know that to understand this story, which is about my setting forth to break the bonds he tied me with."[1] The power her father exerts over Rhoda is regressive: he is the traditional macho male in the South in the 1950s, who continues to want the women in his life to be demure and conservative, to remain unexposed to liberating attitudes about women's rights, and even racial ones. At the novel's beginning, Rhoda, completing her freshman year at Vanderbilt, is informed by her parents that they are moving from where they have been living, in Kentucky, back down to the Deep South. "Back to Alabama where he knows the governor," she tells her roommate, but not with pride. "My daddy's family owns the whole county where they live. So now he's rich and he can go back there."[2] Further, her father is campaigning for her to transfer from Vanderbilt to the University of Alabama; even though a Vanderbilt graduate himself, he finds the place too liberal for Rhoda. And so the transfer is pretty much forced on her. In Tuscaloosa, in the 1950s, so her father feels, Rhoda will be imbued with traditional southern values, particularly southern values necessary for women to honor and practice.

The second pole in Rhoda's life at this time is a young man her own age whom she meets in the Alabama town, Dunleith, to which her parents have now moved, and where she goes to stay the summer between her freshman and sophomore years, between the enlightenment of Vanderbilt and the "Old-South" of the University of Alabama. His name is Charles William Waters, and he is artistic and a free spirit for North Alabama in the 1950s; he is gay, a fact that Rhoda will not find easy to accept but *will* accept, for Charles William answers a need in the young Rhoda: "All my life I had wanted a friend who knew what I was talking about."[3]

Rhoda will be pulled by Charles William in a direction opposite to her father: her entrée into a land of free expression and exposure to creative people with progressive ideas about race relations, but at the same time exposure to the darker side of southern culture in these pre–civil rights times. (Early in the novel, very early in their friendship, Charles William takes Rhoda to a cock fight/Klan meeting, and Rhoda is extremely disturbed by this aspect of her native state; and, done without sensationalism, it is one of the best-drawn, most haunting scenes in the book.)

Rhoda's father wants her to be contained within the white, male-dominated, upper middle-class world he is doing everything possible within his power to preserve and keep inviolate. Although he never actually speaks such words as *"don't rock the boat"* to Rhoda, this sentiment underscores all the words of criticism he *does* level at her. Confined—imprisoned—in this world all summer, "all [Rhoda] did all day was watch the maids take care of the babies and go shopping and walk into the kitchen to see what time it was."[4]

"Some fortunate star, some bright crystalline piece of luck had given me Charles William . . . as counterweight to all of that,"[5] Rhoda recognizes; and he wants to expand Rhoda's universe, lead her to see life outside the rigid social cocoon in which her father is determined to contain her. When he takes Rhoda to meet his cousin and his cousin's wife, Derry, the latter a "Yankee journalist," who live a liberal and liberating existence in Montgomery, Rhoda is stunned to realize "I had never in my life been in a place so charged, so energized. It seemed momentous things were going on around me as dinner was being prepared. It seemed I had waited all my life to be sitting in this room with Derry."[6]

Provocatively, Gilchrist sets up a third but lesser pole of gravitational pull upon Rhoda—a definitely weaker force than her father and her good friend—and this third power is the young man she marries soon after meeting him: Malcolm Martin, Charles William's former roommate at the college they attend in Atlanta. The irony is that Charles William introduces him to Rhoda: the irony being that Charles William loves Rhoda to death, but by introducing Malcolm to her he has set her on a quick path to heartache and despair in the form of a disastrous marriage, a marriage that breaks down almost as soon as it begins, although two adorable sons are produced before its absolute collapse. Malcolm may have come into Rhoda's life because of Charles William, but Malcolm attempts to pull her away from Charles William's bohemian ways; Rhoda's father finds Malcolm a lightweight, and Malcolm attempts to pull her away from his father-in-law's inexorable influence.

But in neither effort is Malcolm successful. The truth is, he stands on the same side as Rhoda's father: his desire for her to be a quiet, acquiescent, even mousy wife of the 1950s South. He is simply a younger generation of the type of southern man typified by Rhoda's father. Both of them despise and attempt to dismiss the progressive attitudes to which Charles William introduces her. Malcolm certainly complicates Rhoda's life negatively, but his power over her is minimal compared to the influence exercised by her father and Charles William; but it is the mess of her marriage that is the primary *materiel* of this novel. That is exactly as it should be, for Malcolm—her marriage to him, specifically—is the playing field, as it were, for Rhoda to gather sufficient bruising to her psyche to ultimately strengthen herself and declare independence from him and, more importantly, from her father as well.

In Malcolm, Rhoda believed she could find the love she never sensed emanating from her big, looming, domineering father; with Charles William having illuminated the way, Rhoda is now on the road to loving herself, the prerequisite, of course, for her to successfully love a man. Now, to be sure, although Rhoda, in the prefatory remarks at the novel's beginning insists that "In the end I got free"[7]—from the dominion of her father, that is—such a process is not actually witnessed. In fact, at novel's end, it is her father who comes to rescue her from the quicksand of her marriage in which she has nearly suffocated. But remarkably—a testament to the complete and careful way Gilchrist has fashioned the character of Rhoda—it is simply *known*, based on the ubiquitous presence of Charles William's influence, that Rhoda *will* make more constructive choices, more independent choices, more satisfactorily adventuresome choices in her life, particularly as these choices apply to men.

What really propels this novel to the top level of Gilchrist's oeuvre is that Gilchrist links the struggle of the New South trying to escape its history to the struggle of Rhoda's turbulent years. She correlates the interior of Rhoda's finding her own personal path to contentment and fulfillment to the exterior of history and current events going on around her. In other words, the outside world functions not simply as a backdrop here but as the actual catalyst for rethinking and action. Rhoda as a little girl did little girl things that have a universality to them regardless of time and place; southern Indiana and Illinois during World War II is solid grounding for her I-want-to-be-just-like-a-boy exploits, but how she was to grow up was not so forged by conditions of setting as by family. In this novel, however, Gilchrist creates a stronger outside effect, which, in turn, creates a stronger interior Rhoda. And this exterior is, of course, the changing mores of the South, from Old South to New South, from an atmosphere of institutionalized racial and female repression to not only dialogue about social changes but also to open defiance of the white patriarchal system. It is an elevation process that Gilchrist handles well, for the novel speaks loudly but not shrilly, neither accusatory nor excusatory toward the South; it places her abiding concern for the evolution of the independent female character within a context that illuminates it in sharp relief—to great effect and to optimal significance and meaning to the reader.

But a review in the *Times Literary Supplement* suggested this general, nonspecific drawback to *Net of Jewels*: "Ellen Gilchrist has yet to put herself together as a writer, formidable though her talent obviously is."[8] And in her previously cited article, "Progress and Perception," Dorie LaRue lobs even stronger criticism at *Net of Jewels*: "The novel sprawls, and Rhoda does not move toward anything in particular. . . . Her indulgence and her spoiled obliviousness ultimately have no point."[9]

Gilchrist's next book was also a novel—but one that very much suffers in comparison to its predecessor. *Starcarbon* was published in 1994, and it cannot fail to disappoint, even if *not* compared to *Net of Jewels*. *Starcarbon* is, simply, an overly busy and tiresome book; in it, Gilchrist's imagination and creativity sag. It is another book about the Hand family: about the brothers, sisters, and nieces of Anna Hand, the famous writer who was the central character of *The Anna Papers*. *Starcarbon* takes place in the summer of 1991, just a few years, then, after Anna Hand's suicide. Her sister Helen, executor of Anna's estate, is living in Boston with Mike, a well-known Irish poet whom Anna had designated in her will as co-executor with Helen. The two had never met prior to coming together to follow Anna's wishes to sort through and organize her papers. Quickly after their first meeting, however, chemistry sizzles, and, as *Starcarbon* opens, Helen has forsaken her husband and children back in Charlotte, North Carolina, and is cohabiting with Mike in such a blissful state she hardly believes her own happiness. The story will have an ending strikingly parallel to how it opens: Mike so engrossed in Helen's stories of her family that, at the end, he is using them as the fabric of a new novel he begins writing.

But the central character here turns out to be Daniel, Helen's and Anna's next-to-youngest brother. (Gilchrist finally supplies a family tree, so all the Hands and the related Manning family can be kept straight.) Daniel has a drinking problem, which has been indicated in previous works about the Hands; and the problem has not abated, nor is he doing well financially, for his tractor business is failing. Also Daniel has had a string of girlfriends since his divorce; after all, as Gilchrist states every chance she can, he remains quite handsome and charming. His latest girlfriend is Margaret, forty-something and hoping for some kind of indication of her future with Daniel—he being the catch that he is, despite his heavy drinking and failing finances.

Daniel's teenage daughter, Jessie, when last seen in the novella "A Summer in Maine" in the collection of novellas *I Cannot Get You Close Enough,* was pregnant by (and having been hastily married to) King, the equally young son of Crystal Manning of New Orleans. At novel's opening, Jessie's baby is due anytime. Jessie and King live in New Orleans, in a house Crystal and her husband Manny, a successful lawyer, bought for them.

Daniel's other daughter, Olivia, the half-Cherokee from Oklahoma, of whose existence Daniel had no idea until, as witnessed in *The Anna Papers,* his sister Anna unearthed her and brought her into the Hand family fold in Charlotte, is finishing her freshman year at the University of North Carolina—and hates it. She feels out of place, that she has nothing in common with these college people; and she intends to spend the summer rejuvenating back in Oklahoma with her Indian family, where, too, lives the boyfriend she left behind a couple years ago when she came East to inaugurate her new life as a well-to-do, socially connected Hand of Charlotte, North Carolina.

The remaining couple—the novel is, after all, subtitled "A Meditation on Love"—that Gilchrist examines in terms of what their relationship consists of—is that between Dr. Georgia Jones and her lover. Georgia has come to the small college in the Oklahoma town that Olivia is from and to which she now has returned, both of whom, Georgia and Olivia, having plans to stay the summer (Georgia teaches anthropology, and she and Olivia become friends when Olivia signs up for her course). Georgia's lover is Zach Biggs, a professor of physics at the University of Arkansas in Fayetteville, and the divorced father of two monstrous boys, and from whom Georgia is currently taking time away for some breathing space.

So, then, the relationships Gilchrist holds up to scrutiny in this novel, inspecting them for truths and strengths and flaws in structure, are these: first, Jessie and King, young parents of a baby boy, but hardly more than children themselves. King attends college and has a difficult time kicking booze and drugs and a teenager's natural sense of irresponsibility; and Jessie is still not completely ready to transfer the-man-in-my-life love from her handsome and still-living-like-he's-rich daddy to her new husband. Second, Olivia and Bobby. She has returned to Oklahoma to find herself again, since discovering her father and going to be with him and his—*her*—family in North Carolina gave her no satisfactory sense of it; and Bobby, the only noble, heroic man in this whole novel, is indeed crazy in love with Olivia and, hearing she is returning to Oklahoma, gives up his very successful and sustaining job as a horse trainer at Starcarbon Ranch in Montana to head back home with the intention of persuading Olivia to marry him. Third, Georgia Jones and Zach Biggs, up to their individual eyebrows in an amazingly dysfunctional relationship (for her it boils down simply to sex, for him down to—who knows?), in which neither party can see above their own neuroses to notice how ridiculous and even life threatening their whole affair is. And fourth, Daniel, whose family finally intervenes and elicits a promise from him to go to a rehabilitation center and dry out, and whose focus on—obsession with—his two daughters' lives, and reluctance to let them grow up now finally broadens out to include notice and even acceptance of the needs of his girlfriend, Margaret, to whom he finally offers a promise of marriage.

In the slightly more than 300 pages of this novel, Gilchrist figuratively kicks each of these relationships' tires to see whether it is a sound investment for the partners; and by that kicking process readers feel the "air pressure" for themselves, and the substantiality or *in*substantiality of the love/sex connection between the partners. But therein lies the fundamental problem of this novel: the reader fails to truly care about the characters—or, to state the condition more accurately, Gilchrist fails to enlist the reader's total concern for the characters, to engage the reader's sympathy and interest in how these characters act and for what reasons. They are not so much unconvincing as downright tiresome. The Hands are powerful people *used* to power, so Anna Hand declared in *The Anna Papers*; but it is too inbred a power now, too inward focused. They are no longer powerful outside the family, a situation epitomized by Daniel, the failing businessman given to drink.

Consequently the Hands turn their need for power, their congenital need to exercise it, on each other. That in and of itself poses no storytelling problem, of course; it sets up, in fact, a dramatic situation easily attractive to the reader's interest. After all, for example, Lillian Hellman's play *The Little Foxes* certainly focused on a powerful southern family that exerted its muscle internally—to the point of internal destruction. Even so, how many times could Hellman bring Regina Giddons and her brothers back onto the stage in successive plays and have the audience extend the hand of interest to them? Characters can be wrung only so much till they are dry; and characters, like real people, have varying numbers of interesting sides to them, varying numbers of events in their lives other people care to hear about. Fortunately, Rhoda and Nora Jane have plenty of compelling aspects and history, but the Hands do not.

Such is the problem of the heavy use of recurrent characters: the risk that readers will tire of them, that the author's conception of them will come to be all drawn out; and trying to keep them new when there is nothing new to be said about them. Obviously, some of Gilchrist's recurrent characters have been conceived with an apparently endless supply of sides and stages that keep readers wanting to come back to them; other of her recurrent characters go nowhere over the long term, simply continuing to spin around in their sameness. Even for Olivia and Jessie, Anna Hand's nieces, by now their authenticity as characters has been ironed out into flatness. Olivia's ambivalence about whether she wants to be in or out of the Hand family cannot sustain such repetition. We, frankly, cannot wait for a final answer from her, not because of great anticipation but because by now we want to get up and leave the room and leave this tired question solely to Olivia.

On the other hand, a review in *Publisher's Weekly* could not disagree more, insisting that Gilchrist, in this book, "writes with a distinctively Southern toughness about people who are selfish, demanding, and often cruel to those closest to them, but who invariably gain the reader's sympathy with their total honesty and fierce need for love."[10]

Gilchrist's next book is also a novel, her third novel in a row. But *Anabasis,* published in 1994 (the same year as *Starcarbon*), is a complete departure from anything she had done before or has done since—at least on the *surface* it represents quite a departure. *Anabasis* (the word is of Greek origin, meaning "an inland march") is a historical novel, set in ancient Greece more than 400 years before the birth of Christ—to set the context more exactly: at the time when the golden age of ancient Greece was sliding into decline. This was a time, as Gilchrist so eloquently identifies it through the words of one of the novel's main characters, "I lived in an age where honor was the chief desire of men and I have lived to see the end of that."[11] Specifically, as the novel opens, Pericles is the ruler of Athens and is "busy fighting a war with the Spartans, a cruel and conservative people who enslaved their kinsmen and sent their sons into the army at an early age."[12] No matter if the shine of classic Greek culture has begun to tarnish in the face of plague and internecine struggles between the major city-states, there still hangs over the peninsula a consciousness of the primacy of Greece in the world.

In the short introduction to *Anabasis,* Gilchrist posits, "This is not a book of history. It is an attempt to tell a story I made up when I was a child."[13] There is no point in insisting otherwise; no point in her word not being taken that the book sprang from a "childhood fantasy." But, nevertheless, because her knowledge of—research into, obviously—the politics and customs of ancient Greece is so impressively complete and gracefully rendered into fiction, this is indeed a history book: a book reconstructing in rich detail a particular historical period. To readers familiar with Gilchrist's previous books, *Anabasis* certainly comes as a surprise, but a pleasant one. This novel boasts every quality that a successful and satisfying novel should have, and which its immediate predecessor *Starcarbon* lacked. And something that none of her novels up to this point possessed: sheer excitement of plot, to the point where the reader is hardly able to turn the pages fast enough to see what twist or turn the plot will take next. Gilchrist can command such thrill as that in many of her short stories, but up to *Anabasis,* it has not been the experience with her novels.

Anabasis rests on two basic and timeless themes: the coming-of-age story and the perilous journey tale. The person who both comes of age and embarks on a perilous journey is named Auria, and she is, as the novel opens, an enslaved adolescent in service in the villa of Meldrus Helonai. The villa is located near Thisbe on the road to Delphi, "on a bluff overlooking the Gulf of Corinth and was a famous trading post known all over the Aegean."[14] In the master's employ is the old man Philokrates, herbalist and alchemist and philosopher; it is to Philokrates that our heroine Auria is apprenticed. He has, in the nine years since her purchase as a slave, taught Auria his knowledge of healing and the physical universe and—probably illegally—how to read and write.

Their boon companion is the dog Metis, who will remain faithful to Auria till advanced age and who, given by Gilchrist a personality all his own (without anthropomorphizing him into ridiculousness), becomes an actual character in his own right.

One day in Auria's and Philokrates' exploration of the woods and caves in the surrounding area, they discovered the remains of an infant that recently had been born to a slave girl in the villa and left to die of hunger and exposure: a foreshadowing of events, and the sight of it, and horrible *idea* of it, haunts Auria for some time.

Meanwhile, a trading partner of Auria's master has come to the villa, and Auria is offered to the guest for a few nights of pleasure—basically, he rapes her. Auria is thus thrust headlong into womanhood, not only with reluctance but also with undying rage. "The memory was all over her, and the smell of incense burning and the smell of his body and the guard's blank eyes. The taste and sound of the things that had been done to her covered her like a caul."[15]

Soon, her great mentor Philokrates dies, and without his protection, not even Auria herself can know how vulnerable she is to the whims of the master of the villa. The answer to the question of what her future may be falls literally into her hands: a baby girl delivered by the mistress of the villa. Auria serves as midwife for the delivery, and when, because the mistress has had only daughters before, the newborn is cast out—taken to a cave to die— Auria knows exactly what she has to do. "Purpose was upon her like a dream of order, like a song. All her decisions were over in a moment's time. After that, all she had to do was act."[16]

And act she does. She packs up some provisions and takes along her dog Metis and the goat Phoebe, who had been like a pet to Philokrates (and who, like the dog, becomes a character herself, without metamorphosis into some kind of glove-wearing, dancing-on-two-feet animal-character one often finds in a children's story); and the three of them flee their home. Auria's mission, of course, is to go the cave where abandoned girl babies are left and rescue this one she had helped deliver, and then somehow create a life for both of them. "I am free. . . . I am not afraid. I am Auria."[17]

She names the baby Kleis, and all the information Philokrates had taught her about resources available in the woods she remembers—in fact, the education about the natural world she received at his knee will stand her in good stead for the rest of her adventurous life. First and foremost, of course, is the need to find food and shelter. The goat supplies the baby with milk; Metis the dog could fend for himself, if necessary, but Auria does not want her companion and protection against both wolf and human intruder to wander too far. Eventually, their directionless flight draws them to what seems like a gift from the gods, for Auria came upon a marvelous sight: stone steps down into a valley where stood a "beautiful little sanctuary,"[18] its obvious perfection as a place to hide and reside not concealed by its overgrowth of vines.

What Auria is unaware of is that this hut was built by a man named Clarius, who is a cousin of the mistress of the villa who gave birth to the baby Auria fled with and has named Kleis. Clarius is now in Athens; he is from a wealthy Athenian family but in youth "had fallen under the spell of philosophers"[19] and led his father's slaves in uprising. At this point in time he is the leader of a movement bent on freeing all the slaves in Atticus, and the movement has "outposts on three islands and two camps in the mountains."[20]

Auria will become deeply involved in this movement, but for the time being she is busy fixing up the sanctuary she was blessed to discover in her flight from her previous life and home. Weeks, then months, go by, the baby growing—as is Auria, who is hardly more than a child herself. And while Kleis naps, Auria practices her writing, a skill she had no intention of allowing to fall into disuse.

Just as Auria begins to desire human contact again, she is discovered in her isolated state by a young man named Meion, who is out scouting in the area from a camp high in the mountains—one of the very camps of runaway slaves who have joined the movement to free all slaves, of which Clarius is leader. This camp is led locally by Leucippius, a man of great stature and a friend of Pericles; but, in a twist in twisted Athenian politics, if Pericles should fall, Leucippius would find a price on his head and his camp at risk of attack and extermination.

Meion takes Auria and the baby Kleis to his camp high up, and Auria experiences with him the "new world of strange sensations and pleasures"[21] that sex with him furnishes, in such incredible contrast to the brutal rape that had been her only previous sexual experience. In fact, after awhile in relatively safe residence in the mountain camp, Auria and Meion exchange vows in a wedding ceremony, their mutual love obvious to all.

So, the first third of the novel followed Auria within the setting in which she grew up—the villa of Medrus Helonai—and in her six-year-long occupancy of the hut in the woods, which she'd literally stumbled upon when running away from home with the baby Kleis; and the last two-thirds of the novel is given over to Auria's encampment high in the mountains—to which she had arrived unaware exactly how much her life would change. Auria makes an impression on Leucippius, the camp leader, and he on her; and we witness Auria, as a member of the camp, isolated as it is, grow in sophistication. "The villa had been a little country farm where they only heard rumors of the world. Now, in this camp, so far away from the settled part of Attica, there seemed to be great things going on."[22]

One thing she had not completely understood was that her new husband, the beautiful and virile Meion, is a warrior first and foremost. "Is this a warrior's life?" she naively asks him.

Indeed it is.

"There is no war up here," she continues innocently.

To which Meion, wiser about the world than she, answers, "There is always war. A man takes territory and defends it."[23]

Over the next few months, Auria will taste the warrior life, coming to the realization that in the outside world, war *is* what men do. But, for the moment, she is part of a lovely domestic arrangement, caught in this brief but indelible word picture: "Auria was seated with Meion beside the hearth. Kleis was asleep beside them in a basket of rushes. Meion had his head in Auria's lap, his foot crossed upon his knee. As he moved his leg the shadows of their bodies played against the wall. Metis [the dog] was near them, curled into a fat red ball. Phoebe [the goat] was against the wall, eating an apple."[24]

But such domestic harmony was not to last long. Unbeknown to Auria, Clarius, the movement's leader, in whose hut Auria had spent time after fleeing the villa where she had been raped, is planning to leave his cover in Athens and join the movement's camp high the mountains. In addition, word comes one day that Meion's mother has been taken captive by hostile forces, which abound in Greece in these days. Meion insists he must go to find her, and quickly he is indeed gone; and despite her loneliness without him, Auria, putting her ability to read and write to good use, begins an academy for the children of the camp so they too may benefit from literacy.

Clarius, the famous Clarius, does indeed arrive at the camp, and he and Auria establish a bond. She enlists herself as his disciple; and for his part Clarius declares, "You made my heart young, Auria."[25]

But still no word from Auria's beloved Meion. On the other hand, news *does* reach them that the great Athenian leader Pericles is dead, and in his place now rule two generals who undoubtedly will send forces to attack the mountain camp, which, as they know, has been "an irritation" to one of the generals for years.

Meion arrives back at the camp safe and sound, and, soon afterward his mother finds her way there, too. A siege is prepared for, and, as one of the preparations, Auria takes the children of the camp higher up into the mountains to hide in caves. Battle ensues, but Auria and Meion survive—in the epilogue, in fact, three years have passed, and they live in a house they have built near the hut Auria had found refuge in, hopefully far enough away from the fracas still defining in Greek politics.

Anabasis is, purely and simply, a historical novel, and so it must be judged by the standards of that genre. Historical fiction's "function" can be defined as an occasion for didacticism and not simply an occasion for an author to portray personal responses to life's multifarious events and conditions, however esthetically rendered that portrayal may be. This latter circumstance, of course, is non-genre fiction's only obligation. Historical fiction, on the other hand, must *do* more and *be* more. A good historical novel must be good fiction, but also *more*.

Historical novels must teach; they must transport readers, accurately and naturally, back to the past. The more accurate the transportation the better. And the more natural, more comfortable, smoother the transportation, also the better. That means that the didactic aspect of historical fiction must be well integrated into the plot; historical details must *support* the story rather than intrude and distract from its exposition. Successful historical novelists have done their research more than just barely, they have done it *thoroughly*; but then, in turn, they do not lecture the reader on their informational discoveries. No successful historical novelist tosses big chunks of researched but undigested information into the narrative, to sit as lumps that act as obstructions the reader must spend time and energy navigating around, like icebergs to ocean liners.

By that rule *Anabasis* must be judged an excellent historical novel. Gilchrist's understanding of ancient Grecian history, politics, and customs—down to food and drink—is thorough. From how they dressed to how they fought in battle, all features of life at that time and place are presented with great knowledge, but also with considerable liquidity. This novel is no dry history lecture delivered from a podium; it is a well-researched but also well-imagined, well-balanced evocation that *arises* from historical knowledge on the author's part, knowledge that has become second nature to her. Not regurgitated facts drawn from an encyclopedia, but a real world shaped in authenticity and with a writerly talent for the telling and colorful but not overburdensome detail: such is the characteristic of the successful historical novel, and such is *Anabasis*.

Ironically, how much better the reader gains a sense of ancient Greece from reading *Anabasis* than of contemporary Charlotte, North Carolina, from reading the two Hand novels. Historical novels are a dime a dozen, most done quite amateurishly. This one, however, is exceptional. That said, something *else* must be said: how well *Anabasis* succeeds as a novel, period. We had introduced our discussion of it by saying what a departure it was for Gilchrist—at least on the surface. Obviously, the surface is ancient Greece, most definitely a unique setting for her. But in an important way, *Anabasis* is very much like all of Gilchrist's fiction: the connecting factor being her depiction of a strong female protagonist, a depiction here, as in her other successful novels, and in nearly all of her short stories, deriving from her instinct for the ambivalence (mostly toward men) of women who are forceful and self-determining, their ambivalence about power and independence being the very material of their realism and honesty as characters.

With Auria, Gilchrist shares one of her richest—yes, too, exotic—understandings of the strong female protagonist. (Even the intrepid Nora Jane Whittington seems less decisive and assertive in comparison.) When Auria flees the villa in which she grew up, in her arms the baby girl she rescued, it is done with no certain idea where to go. The path—the *literal* path—she sets out on branches in two at one point, leaving her with a dilemma—"Which shall I take, she wondered, staring up the mountain, waiting for a sign."—but then only a second later it dawns on her "*I am the sign*. I am the one who chooses." That could be a banner Auria flies, on it written "I am the sign. I am the one who chooses."[26] But Auria is neither an oddball nor a misanthrope; mistress of her own destiny means for her, to use a contemporary expression, working within the system. Her years alone with just the child—just the child as *human* company, that is—as they restore to habitability the hut she finds in the woods—eventually come to remind her that being alone is fine up to a point, but people eventually need to regain society, if for no other reason than not to forget how to communicate. Even though at one point in her state of aloneness, Auria insists to herself, "I fear nothing. Not even loneliness. I am hardened by the loneliness. . . . I will kill loneliness, I will never go back"[27]; even though at one time she subscribed to that sentiment, by the time Meion discovers her at the hut, her current observation is that "only animals live alone."[28]

This theme of loneliness—specifically, the fear of it and the attempts to alleviate it, or in Auria's situation and with her abilities, the successful strategies to alleviate it—is shared with Gilchrist's previous novel, *Starcarbon*. Such a theme is a gift to the reader, for who among us have not the facility and experience to identify with loneliness and its almost-partner: the strength to prevent or relieve it? Handed such an automatic reason for empathy as this, then, why does Auria seize our attention, while the plight of the Hand family of the previous novel leaves us unstirred? Wouldn't a quicker and more intimate response to contemporary people living in North Carolina and Oklahoma make more sense than to ancient people living in classical Greece?

Not if the main character is Auria. She is respectable; her strength is admirable, and her desire for freedom and her final choice *not* to be alone are completely comprehensible. Unlike the Hands, Auria was not born into privilege, and in contrast to the reaction it is so easy to feel about her, it is difficult to feel compassion for the Hands' whininess. Auria pulls herself up and assumes control of her problems; her issues have authenticity to a person of her time, age, and gender. When comparing her to the two young Hand half-sisters, Jessie and Olivia, the only response suitable to those two young women is the contemporary expression "Get over yourselves!"

But, of course, critical response to the novel has its negative aspects as well; for example, in this review in the *New York Times Book Review,* which found that it "bogs down in exposition. Its long-ago-and-far-away style dulls the reader's attention. This fan [the reviewer, that is] admired much of the novel, but wished Ms. Gilchrist had written it with the same energy she displays in her present-day stories about Rhoda and Traceleen."[29] And *Kirkus* insisted that the novel is a "bland tale," that "Auria is never a credible character," calling her a "saintly bore."[30]

Chapter 8

Hitting Her Stride in Stories and Novels (*Age of Miracles, Rhoda, Courts of Love, Sarah Conley*)

GILCHRIST'S NEXT BOOK, which was published in 1985, is a collection of stories—16 in number—titled *The Age of Miracles*. Fresh from the reading experience of her novel *Anabasis*, an extremely accomplished novel and a particularly noteworthy *historical* novel, gears are shifted from novel to short story, from, in terms of setting, ancient Greece to the contemporary American South—the latter a return, of course, to Gilchrist's familiar milieu.

The Age of Miracles, her sixth book of short stories, showcases Gilchrist's outstanding traits as a fiction writer and how well the short story form distills these strengths. As much as *Anabasis* and, before that, *Net of Jewels,* demonstrated a step to a more secure level of conception and execution of the novel, the stories in *The Age of Miracles* suggest a conclusion in the opposite direction: that Gilchrist draws on her talents more effectively, more poignantly, more intelligently, and more artistically in the short form. At this point in our examination and appreciation of her fiction, we face the fact that Gilchrist writing *in concentration* is actually the more muscled side of her ability.

Half of the 16 stories feature the recurrent character Rhoda Manning. Also, intrepid but never overbearing Nora Jane Whittington, another recurrent Gilchrist character, appears in one story. And two stories bring back that feisty duet of Crystal Manning of New Orleans and her maid, the ever-wise and typically unflappable Traceleen. An important question this collection poses is, are these recurrent characters worthy of further exploration, or has Gilchrist used them to the point of exhausting reader interest in them?

In answer, the most satisfying aspect of her use of recurrent characters—the Hand family notwithstanding—is how tiresome they *do not* become. An occasional story in this collection may falter a little, suddenly ring somewhat lifeless, but that infrequent occurrence stems more from the unexciting circumstances into which Gilchrist has *placed* the character rather than from repetition of the character herself. Gilchrist continues to show that there are apparently endless ways in which Rhoda Manning can be observed, from girlhood to middle age, which affords wider and deeper observations of her character. As far as Nora Jane, Crystal, and Traceleen are concerned, encountering them again in this collection can only be experienced as a pleasure.

Exactly what is observable about Rhoda in these stories that extends a fuller comprehension of her as a character? The first story in the collection, "A Statue of Aphrodite," presents the adult Rhoda in the year 1986. The very young Rhoda continues to be a delight—her juvenile independence and even insolence quite amusing and even exciting—and equally delightful is the fully mature, stepping-into-middle-age Rhoda. The young married Rhoda, with young sons, is the characterization of her that is her most obnoxious: selfish and self-centered nearly to the point of cruelty toward the people around her. This collection only sustains and supports these ideas. This first story in the collection, Rhoda appearing in vivid color, presents this picture of her: She has, by now, made a good reputation for herself as a writer and moved from Fayetteville, Arkansas, back to live with her folks in Jackson, Mississippi, "riding out the AIDS scare by being an old maid and eating dinner nearly every night with [her] parents."[1] But Rhoda meets a handsome physician—is a celibate Rhoda imaginable for very long?—when she travels to Atlanta to do a staff enrichment program at his hospital. Rhoda obviously has not changed in one regard since she was a little girl trying to be let in on her brothers' activities: that is, of course, how much her sense of self and her equilibrium are at the mercy of male attention. And in the story "A Wedding in Jackson," Rhoda is now in her late fifties and, although still very much aware of men and the importance of their place in her life, she is now exhibiting a middle-aged perspective on the issue of men. In this first-person narrative about, as the title suggests, Rhoda attending a family wedding, she admits that she has mellowed.

On the other side of the coin, Rhoda is at her "worst"—her most egotistical and nasty—in the shocking story "The Stucco House." The protagonist is actually Teddy, a child in the second grade, who is called on to help his stepfather, Eric, whom we understand Teddy adores, to go gather up Teddy's drunk and passed-out mother from another night of her revelries; and three-fourths of the way through the narrative, it is made shockingly clear that this alcoholic, delusional, truth-abusive woman is none other than Rhoda.

Her marriage to Eric has indeed failed by the time this particular plot line is picked up again in "Going to Join the Poets." Teddy is now a teenager and involved in drugs. This is, of course, as witnessed before, the period in Rhoda's life during which her personality traits manifest themselves least admirably—even intolerably. She neglects what she should be paying attention to—her marriage and children—to focus solely on her own needs: which, at this point in time and in this particular story, means obsessing over finding what she really wants in life—*out* of life—that would make *her* happy and complete, a state to which Rhoda has not yet arrived, has yet to experience. Here Rhoda has decided that as a writer she will achieve fame; as a poet, she would "have her name in lights, to be famous, lauded and beloved."[2] These are, almost inarguably, shallow, hollow goals—ones formulated by a person who has never been loved enough. But of course, that is how Rhoda presents herself in this period of her life: shallow, hollow, and obsessed with being loved, but seeking love from the wrong sources. Fame will indeed come to Rhoda in middle age, the vehicle for it, her writing talent; and having achieved her goal of her "name in lights" ironically allows Rhoda the mellowness found in the stories about her in her later years. In essence, then, Rhoda can afford the last laugh. *See?* she can exclaim to the world. I *did* it!

But, ultimately, Rhoda's transitions reflect real life. It can be argued that Rhoda's life is indeed a paradigm: that the period in a person's life from twenties to, say, early forties, from the time of leaving youth to the point of arriving at middle age, often represents the testing years, the yearning years, the striving years, which can amount to the most trying time for the people around them. Achieving such realism in her depiction of female characters distinguishes Gilchrist's fiction first and foremost.

Her realistic portrayal—her accurate understanding—of female characters is also in evidence in the other stories in this collection. "The Blue House" is a backstory to Nora Jane Whittington's life at age 14, an earlier depiction of her life than any previous encounter. Nora Jane has not extended the pleasure of her company since four books ago, since the short story collection *Light Can Be Both Wave and Particle*. But soon into this new Nora Jane story, the assertion that "When she was about four years old Nora Jane . . . decided to be strong" brings the almost comforting reappreciation that Nora Jane is admirable for her strength, that she is unburdened by self-centeredness, self-destructiveness, and manipulativeness that comprise the ingredients of Rhoda's strength—which is often simply defiance rather than actual strength. Nora Jane's inner resources and genial nature come to the fore in "The Blue House." Nora Jane is happy spending time at her grandmother's house in New Orleans but not so eager to have to go back home to her mother's house, just a few blocks away, for her mother sinks deeper into alcoholism. But when her grandmother dies, Nora Jane no longer has that important—life sustaining, really—refuge. What will she do? Live all the time with her mother? Her mother swears off alcohol but can live up to the promise for only a few short days. Yet Nora Jane's resolve to preserve herself at any cost, despite adverse conditions hitting her square in the face, is only strengthened when she realizes, in precocious maturity, that "I don't have to pay any attention to her [her mother]. All I have to do is go to school and wait to get out of here. I'll get out sooner or later. That's for sure."[3] And, of course, Nora Jane has already shown, in the stories about her appearing thus far, that she does indeed break free of her mother's illness and proceed to create a life for herself.

Another recurrent character—actually a duet of characters, for these two always appear together—is Crystal Manning of New Orleans and her black maid, Traceleen; and another of the delightful Crystal-as-viewed-by-Traceleen stories, is "Too Much Rain, or, The Assault of the Mold Spores." Again, how easy and comfortable it is to snuggle into a charming Traceleen story. This time out, it seems Crystal has developed allergies, and consequently, to fight against mold spores, lots of the furnishings and decorations of the house are removed. Of course the always wise Traceleen is not without an opinion on the subject. "You cannot win at this allergy game. Once your body goes autoimmune on you, it is just one long trip to the doctor or the drugstore."[4] Crystal's husband Manny decides to send them to Florida—Crystal, Traceleen, and Crystal's daughter—to give Crystal a good opportunity to get over her allergy attack; and, indeed, once there, Crystal insists the salt air is doing her no end of good.

But certainly in one respect Crystal is *not* a new woman by the sea: in her reaction to the presence of a handsome man, that is. As Traceleen confides, "I have seen Miss Crystal get that way before, like she has seen a way out of a tunnel that she thought had no end. Like she had been asleep for days and all of a sudden woke up and started blinking."[5] But the handsome man poses no real threat to Crystal's marriage, for Traceleen insists Crystal and Manny love each other and "are smart enough for each other and can make each other laugh."[6] Obviously good and sincere bases for a successful marriage.

Crystal makes another appearance in a story called "The Raintree Street Bar and Washerteria," which is rather a throwaway piece about New Orleans society women getting involved in the city's active poetry community—dabbling in the arts, as it were. Crystal is one of these society ladies, and the depiction of her is not a happy one. The only interesting feature of the story is that Sandy Wade is part of the poetry community—Sandy, of course, being Nora Jane's boyfriend, whom she follows to California to begin her new life there. Thus two of Gilchrist's recurrent characters, Crystal and Nora Jane, heretofore not brought within an inch of one another, have one degree of separation in this story. But it is mostly a gimmick, to be appreciated only by readers familiar with all of Gilchrist's work.

In "Madison at 69th, a Fable," Gilchrist proves once again the effectiveness of the attention-ensnaring opening for a short story. "There were four people in on the kidnapping, although only three of them were kin to the victim, and the fourth really shouldn't be held accountable since she was in love. The fourth is me."[7] Clearly, an enticement to read on.

"A Wedding in Jackson" is a Rhoda story I have previously discussed, but, in a second look, evidence is found of another Gilchrist fictional characteristic: the limpid sheerness of her style, particularly her descriptive power when painting verbal pictures of *place*. As an example, as Rhoda is driving from Arkansas to Mississippi, "I turned right onto Highway 454 and the vast fields of the Delta were all around me. The place that I call home. I passed the house built on top of an Indian mound. To my left were plowed fields, flat and verdant, waiting for seed. On my right were the dense woods of Leroy Percy Park, where I was taken for picnics as a child. I turned onto the River Road, Highway 1, famed in literature and legends."[8]

Also in this story, Gilchrist offers a creative solution to her recurrent point of view problem of shifting the perspective from one character to another—but doing so too abruptly. Too often, as has been pointed out, these point of view shifts are simply too jarring, momentarily derailing the story and blunting its effect. But in "A Wedding in Jackson," Gilchrist avoids the problem in this fashion: as Rhoda travels from Fayetteville to Jackson, she imagines her mother waiting for her, but rather than shifting the point of view back and forth from daughter to mother and risking dulling the story's edge, Gilchrist actually intensifies its effect by Rhoda saying to herself, "If I were writing this as a play, I would begin in my mother's house on

Woodwind Lane in Jackson, Mississippi, where she is waiting for me to come and take her to the wedding."[9] And so, as Rhoda draws nearer to her destination, she imagines every so often what her mother is doing and thinking. This technique is not exactly the same as a complete shift in point of view to another character, for, of course, Rhoda's imagined reactions on the part of her mother are still from her own perspective—she is in essence holding up a mirror to herself to guess how others see her. Regardless, the device broadens the situation more smoothly than a neck-wrenching point of view shift. This way of seeing herself in a two-person dramatic piece, while another indication of Rhoda's narcissism, nevertheless deepens *our* view of her.

A review in the *Chicago Tribune* felt that Rhoda is, like her parents find, often too overwhelming, at least for the good of this book, insisting that "*The Age of Miracles* is not a collection in which every story works, and one of the flaws is that Rhoda's shadow envelopes nearly every other character."[10]

Gilchrist's next book, *Rhoda: A Life in Stories,* was published in 1995, the same year as *The Age of Miracles.* It is, as the rather prosaic but to-the-point title suggests, a compilation of all the Rhoda Manning stories so far, numbering 22—and with the addition of an excerpt from the Rhoda novel, *Net of Jewels.* And two stories make their debut in book form here.

The question is, is a compilation of all the Rhoda stories (with the exclusion of the dreary "Stucco House" from *The Age of Miracles*) beneficial? The answer is, indeed it is, for Rhoda is—and postponing such a conclusion on my part seems unnecessary—Gilchrist's major achievement, her most obvious, prominent legacy to American letters. An entire book about Rhoda obviously exists, of course: the previously discussed novel *Net of Jewels.* But the novel's time frame, in terms of Rhoda's life, is limited to her college and young womanhood, and the compilation of Rhoda stories gives an expanded picture: from girlhood to middle age.

This expanded picture that the short story compilation extends is achieved in mosaic fashion, of course; a story collection, even one bound as tightly as this one by its focus on a single character, cannot gain the seamlessness, the smoothness, of presentation that a novel can accomplish. Ultimately, however, the difference is moot. Simply, there is a Rhoda novel and an all-Rhoda collection of stories, neither one redundant, and both contribute to Gilchrist's oeuvre-wide depiction of this character. But a second question about this gathering of the Rhoda stories is, can—and how does—Rhoda develop as a character from one story to the next, when placed, as they are here, in chronological order—not by year of publication but in order of their chronological place in Rhoda's life? In her introduction, Gilchrist relates that she "invented Rhoda Manning on a beautiful fall day in New Orleans,"[11] and, while she has gone on to write many stories about her, Gilchrist admits "Many are true to the real essence of Rhoda I created on that fall morning. Others miss the mark."[12]

What, then, is this "essence" of Rhoda about which Gilchrist speaks? Also in her introduction, she defines the original conception of Rhoda as, "There are no shadows in Rhoda. Rhoda is passion, energy, light."[13] Gilchrist is being unnecessarily difficult on herself with the comment about missing the mark. She shows different Rhodas, yes, but there are simply different *sides* to Rhoda. If "passion, energy, light" represented Gilchrist's original view—conception—of Rhoda Manning, then she never really has missed the mark.

To reiterate a point previously made, Rhoda is likable best in childhood and middle age and least likable in the years in between, when the passion and energy are present but the light is a little dimmer. Gilchrist also remarks in the introduction, "The one thing I do know is that something wonderful happens to me when I am writing about Rhoda, especially Rhoda as a child."[14] This is obviously an instance of a writer writing about what she *should* be writing about, affirming the cliché "writing about what one knows."

One question remains concerning this compilation of Rhoda stories. What do the two Rhoda stories appearing here that have never been placed in any previous collection contribute to the composite picture of Rhoda? One called "Blue Satin," about Rhoda as a girl, set in southern Illinois (where many previous stories about the child Rhoda have been set); although unmentioned in this particular story, previous ones about her as a little girl have indicated that while World War II rages in the outside world, the Manning family has come North because Rhoda's father is involved in civilian war work. The story's basic premise, as well as a quick identification-check of Rhoda, is supplied by the first sentence: "Rhoda's most easily manipulated grandmother had come to stay with Rhoda and her brothers while Rhoda's parents went off to a football game in Lexington, Kentucky."[15] Of course, "easily manipulated" would indeed be the primary standard by which Rhoda would judge a person. At any rate, her father gave Rhoda 25 dollars before he and Rhoda's mother left town, the cash given to her for emergency use only, in case she or her grandmother happen to need something. Not surprisingly, Rhoda spends it on an indulgence: a blue satin cocktail dress. And she is 12!

Understandably, her grandmother hits the ceiling, but Rhoda is perplexed at the reaction. "There was no end to the insanity of grown people, especially her mother's people from the Delta."[16] Rhoda is forced to return the dress and get her money back. Her grandmother phones Rhoda's parents and insists, "I can't handle her." Her grandmother considered her a "bad little girl to begin with,"[17] and now this. Rhoda, meanwhile, has taken refuge underneath her four-poster bed and smugly amuses herself, away from the outside world, of which she has yet to gain a workable knowledge; but being Rhoda, she really doesn't care, for the world must accommodate itself to her, not vice versa.

And that is, of course, Rhoda's philosophy throughout her life, as emphasized by this gathering of all the Rhoda stories. The conclusion drawn from the Rhoda collection, particularly with this story that had not appeared in any previous collection in mind, is the same conclusion drawn from previous collections that include Rhoda stories: that Rhoda's character traits—chiefly among them, stubbornness, selfishness, and propensity for manipulation—while acceptably muted in middle age, tiresome to an exasperating degree in her years as youngish wife and mother, are most acceptable, even charming, in her childhood. This compilation is a testament to the Rhoda-as-child stories being Gilchrist's signature work. (The second Rhoda story appearing here in book form for the first time, "Drunk Every Day," finds Rhoda at age 26, "at the height of [her] wildness and [her] powers,"[18] married, but charming attractive men, since her "marriage is irrelevant in the larger scheme of things."[19] But a horrible incident happening to her friend sends Rhoda literally back into her husband's arms; and this story becomes rather a layering of the Rhoda character, just an incident—an instance—of her tiresome perfidiousness.)

The book that followed *Rhoda: A Life in Stories* was also a collection of stories, titled *The Courts of Love*, published in 1996. The first nine stories (out of a total of 18) are a sequence featuring another one of Gilchrist's much-loved recurrent female protagonists, Nora Jane Whittington. Nora Jane's last appearance occurred in "The Blue House" in the collection *The Age of Miracles*. That story, it will be remembered, supplied the backstory to the series of California adventures Nora Jane has gotten involved in: in it Nora Jane was only a teenager and having to deal by herself with an alcoholic mother.

So, then, the saga of Nora Jane is picked up again here in *The Courts of Love*, and she is now age 29. Her twin girls are 10, and her husband Freddy

Harwood is 41. Nora Jane has blossomed into a fully mature, wise, and loving and caring adult, which is made obvious again and again in this
sequence. (Her maturity-beyond-her-years and her ingenuity were undis-
guised upon first encounter with her in "The Famous Poll at Jody's Bar" in
Gilchrist's first story collection, *In the Land of Dreamy Dreams*; for even
though the stunt she pulled in that story, a robbery, was not the most legal or
ethical thing she ever would do, it "needed" to be done for her own good.)
Nora Jane, as has been previously posited, is a far more likable character than
Rhoda Manning. This sequence of stories about Nora Jane sets up interesting
contrasts with the all-Rhoda collection of stories, for comparison of Gilchrist's
vision of these two characters, the two about whom she most often writes.

A review of Nora Jane's background, some refresher information, then,
seems advisable at this point. She is living in Berkeley, California, having
gone west several years ago to rendezvous with Sandy, the boyfriend she had
back home in New Orleans. Sandy comes in and out of her life, appears and
disappears; his unsteadiness has little appeal for the increasingly stable and
future-oriented Nora Jane, who marries adorable, upstanding, heroic Freddy,
owner of an independent bookstore in Berkeley, but rich from family money.
Nora Jane lives well with Freddy, with every creature comfort and with a
sensual, sexual, rewarding love between them. The twin girls, Lydia and
Tammili, are only fraternal twins, for unbeknown to them or to Sandy (but
information that is known by Nora Jane and Freddy), Lydia is Sandy's child
and Tammili is Freddy's; at the time of their conception, Nora Jane was
sleeping with both men. (Freddy, befitting the noble, generous man that he
is, makes no distinction in his profound love of and pride in the two girls.)

This sequence of Nora Jane stories actually has a title of its own: "Nora
Jane and Company." Appropriately titled it is, for Gilchrist extends her can-
vas wide here, limning the players in Nora Jane's world as that world stands
at this very successful, happy point in her life. In addition to Nora Jane, there
is Freddy Harwood, of course, and their twin girls; a "supportive" and decid-
edly delightful recurrent character debuting in this story sequence, Freddy's
best friend Nieman; and later in the sequence there is also Stella, Nieman's
new girlfriend, and very quickly his bride; and various interesting "guest"
characters who make, while not recurrent, certainly vivid, appearances. All
the characters, the new ones as well as old friends, tightly connect the
sequence into a whole. However, not one of the stories in which they appear
can hold its own as an individual, freestanding piece. None has a separate,
discreet, and complete meaning individually. It is these particular stories'

totality that is their importance; their combined effect is what matters in terms of their development of the characterization of Nora Jane. Together they constitute what really is a novella with distinct chapters.

The major theme explored here is personal safety. These stories are basically about safeguarding oneself from physical, emotional, and financial harm; and, an extension of that, about safeguarding one's loved ones from such threats. Nora Jane is the epitome of self-protection and protector of the people important in her life. In the opening story, "Perhaps a Miracle," the safety motif is very explicit: Nora Jane and Freddy rescue the little boy next door from drowning in their backyard swimming pool. The boy is visiting next door, having been dumped on his grandmother for babysitting purposes while his actress mother completes filming on location down in Southern California. In the way Gilchrist has of weaving her recurrent characters in and out of other recurrent characters' stories, the boyfriend of the little boy's mother is a fellow actor, none other than Sandy Wade, Nora Jane's boyfriend back in New Orleans, whom she followed to California in the first place—and who is, unbeknown to him, the actual father of one of the Nora Jane's fraternal twin daughters. (Sandy has always been presented in the Nora Jane stories as a shallow individual; even now, his goals remain superficial: "His main desire was to get a good night's sleep so he would be beautiful for the cameras in the morning.")[20]

The story's "independence"—its viability as a freestanding piece away from the others in the sequence—is more than just compromised by the ending; it is absolutely nullified. For the ending is just a shift to Sandy's place in Los Angeles where he lives with the actress mother of the little boy who fell into Nora Jane and Freddy's pool, as he and the woman make plans to drive up to San Francisco and, with definite reluctance on her part, relieve her mother of the stress of caring for her son. The ending, then, is merely an ellipsis. Not that every short story, of course, needs a concrete, complete, airtight drawing in at the end; but this one actually functions to *introduce* another situation rather than conclude the one at hand, and the new situation it leads into actually will be taken up, in a sort of postponement, not by the very next story but by one later in the sequence.

Meanwhile, the story that *is* next in order of appearance, "Lunch at the Best Restaurant in the World," introduces a major-minor character in the sequence: Nieman Gluuk, Freddy's best friend since childhood, and currently an "esteemed and feared" movie critic.[21] The story is brief, in two scenes: set in the restaurant Chez Panisse, where Nora Jane, Freddy, and Nieman are having lunch, and then an hour after the end of lunch, on the Berkeley campus, where Nora Jane has enrolled as a student, and Freddy and Nieman have decided to take some classes, too, just to keep their hands—minds—involved in the current state of the world's knowledge about everything. (Freddy and Nieman attended the university back when they were of the usual college age.)

The story is really only a bridge; this day is the first occasion that the Harwoods had been out in public since the night Nora Jane pulled the little boy from next door from their swimming pool. Their realization from that incident—that the cliché about life's being short bears absolute truth—is what prompts Freddy and his friend to enroll in classes and challenge their minds anew.

Again, this story has little to say on its own, but rather functions as a plot transition, much like a chapter in a book; its purpose is to introduce Nora Jane's latest admirable self-improvement step—getting a college education, which is, of course, a riff on the sequence's major theme of personal security—as well as to introduce Nieman, who will appear regularly in succeeding stories in the sequence.

In the following story, "The Incursions of the Goddamn Wretched Past," Nora Jane, as the title indicates, is faced with a disturbing feature of her previous life—back when she first came to California from New Orleans, that is—that now rears its head, threatening to not so much disturb as *destroy* the life of happiness and security she has taken pains to create for herself. What rears its head—or, more accurately, *who* rears *his* head—is Sandy Wade, Nora Jane's old boyfriend, who is now an actor in L.A. and "ten years older and stronger looking and wider and twelve times as handsome, if it were possible for anyone that handsome to look any better." His stunning looks aside, Sandy is "on his way to San Francisco to ruin [Nora Jane's] life."[22]

This, then, is the story that has picked up the story line laid down at the end of the first story in the sequence. Sandy is, as was learned in that story, the boyfriend of the mother of the little boy who fell into Nora Jane and Freddy's pool, and now in this follow-up story Sandy is coming with the boy's mother up to San Francisco to retrieve him. And the grandmother who is taking care of the boy lives right next to the Harwoods! The plot thickens—for although Sandy is not aware that he is the father of one of Nora Jane's twins, Nora Jane and Freddy realize that if he lays eyes on his daughter, which could easily happen now, it may well be quite obvious to him that *his* face is reflected in *hers*. The problem is, too, that the woman next door informs Nora Jane and Freddy that her daughter, when she gets there, will definitely want to meet and thank Nora Jane and Freddy for the rescue of her son.

In other words, contact between Sandy and *his* child appears likely. And how do Nora Jane and Freddy know that the next-door neighbor's daughter's boyfriend is Sandy? Before Sandy's and the boy's mother's arrival, the next-door lady shows them some recent photographs of him, and there to their absolute shock is Sandy's face.

Nora Jane, particularly with Freddy at her side, is nothing if not strong and resourceful—and protective. "Lonely little only child that she had been, always up in trees with a cat, spinning worlds she could inhabit without fear. Now, into this world she had created with this man, a real world of goodness and light, peace and hope, came this moment and they must bear it and survive it."[23]

Nora Jane and Freddy's solution is drastic but effective: they immediately, within hours, buy a new house and move out of their old one. And the "procedure" works, for off Sandy goes, back to L.A., with his girlfriend and her little boy. Nora Jane has the perfect partner in preserving the peace and serenity of their twin girls' lives in husband Freddy, who, at story's end, "walked out onto the patio and looked up at the stars and started making deals. Just keep them safe, he offered. That's all. Name your price. I'm ready. Don't I always keep my word? Have I ever let you down?"[24] Freddy is, as I have indicated before, the best drawn of all of Gilchrist's male characters, certainly the most heroic.

In fact, Freddy's family protection mind-set is the basis of the next story, "On the Problem of Turbulence." It will be recalled that Freddy owns a bookstore, and as this story opens he is sitting at his desk, reflecting on the past and future. "My Nora, he thought, my life, my hope, my meaning. Freddy Harwood adored his wife and children. He loved them in a manner that seems old-fashioned in a cynical world. He lived to serve and protect them."[25] Freddy will be called on to serve and protect his family to a greater extent than ever before; in fact, this story sports the exciting pace and turns of a thriller novel.

Freddy's bookstore is playing host to a famous editor ("the grand old man of publishing")[26] and his live-in companion, novelist Adrien Searle ("the feared feminist writer")[27], of the latter of whom Nora Jane is a big fan. In fact Nora Jane spends the evening before rereading all of Adrien's books. But something else occupies Nora Jane's mind as well: she is pregnant. It has been her desire, over the years since the birth of the twins, to get pregnant again, but it had not happened; and in the meantime, of course, as observed in a previous story in this sequence, she has enrolled at Berkeley and begun her college education. "The minute you forget about wanting something it shows up"[28]—she posits, in reference to her unplanned but certainly not unwanted pregnancy.

Freddy is ecstatic when she tells him the important news—an anticipated reaction from the noble family man that Freddy has been shown to have become. In addition to this new element in Nora Jane's and Freddy's life together, the novelist Adrien Searle has promised to introduce Nora Jane, who, as it turns out, possesses a beautiful singing voice, to a local opera star. But a member of a Muslim fundamentalist group murders Adrien ("the whore") in her hotel room the morning of Nora Jane's appointment with the singer. And an especially gruesome murder it is, too. (Actually, her murder was a mistake; the group was actually after her publisher boyfriend, publisher of Salmon Rushdie.) Not long after the horrible act, a man harasses one of Nora Jane's and Freddy's twin daughters just outside their house. A connection? Minutes after that, a bomb explodes in Freddy's bookstore. The result of all this is the police placing the two of them and their girls under protection. Nora Jane's own streak of self- and family-protectiveness can't possibly go unexerted, naturally, so she insists on helping with the official interrogation. How all these events are interrelated—or not—is slowly (but carefully, *not* ploddingly) sorted out in what amounts to an exciting narrative. Gilchrist has provocatively and successfully broadened a domestic tale out into the larger universe of contemporary global issues—specifically, reactionary responses to religious differences.

As previously identified, the primary theme running through this sequence of Nora Jane stories is personal safety, each story working out the theme in its own fashion. At the same time, all these Nora Jane stories share a spirited tone differentiating them from the Rhoda Manning sequence, *Rhoda: A Life in Stories.* Nora Jane and Freddy believe in a higher good. They address their lives not so much to the needs of God—whose existence Rhoda flatly denies at every turn throughout her life—as to self-improvement and improvement of others' lives—the latter pursued without obnoxious self-righteousness or tiresome meddlesomeness. Rhoda, as has been repeatedly observed, is simply out for herself; even as an adult, husbands and children always come in a distant second with her. Nora Jane is different, as this sequence of Nora Jane stories progresses, as Gilchrist further molds Nora

Jane into finer detail, an individual emerges who has been blessed with love for herself, and who is consequently able to give it to others and receive it back. There is nothing romantic *or* sarcastic in Gilchrist's endowment of Nora Jane with this "heavenly" gift; it is human and humanizing, adding a dimension to Nora Jane that is missing in Rhoda, and it certainly contributes, because it *is* such a natural and unsentimental quality of Nora Jane's, to the reader's increasing partiality toward the adult Nora Jane over the adult Rhoda.

In tandem with this spirituality is an intriguing scientific aspect to the Nora Jane stories that also keeps them separate from the Rhoda stories. In the introduction to this Nora Jane sequence, Gilchrist forecasts this circumstance that: "the fathers of the twin girls Tammili and Lydia Whittington meet again."[29] (Which, of course, as we have seen, comes true.) Gilchrist goes on, in this introduction, to suggest "one would think this was inevitable. Their DNA [Sandy's and Freddy's] had swum together for nine months, hands touching, legs embracing. In many ways they [Sandy and Freddy] are closer to each other than either of them is to the mother."[30]

Gilchrist, in common with most southern fiction writers, shoulders a deeply felt family consciousness, meaning that her characters never shed their awareness of the social web of which they are a part, as a consequence of their membership in their particular family; a web to be enjoyed and taken advantage of or to give personal grief and be revolted against—often a combination of both reactions comes into play. Nor do they shed, as much as they may attempt to kick over the traces of this restraint on their freedom of thought and action, their awareness of their original place in their families and how much families expect individual members to continue playing their same role into adulthood. But this awareness, those proscriptions, are generally always psychological. What is new in the Nora Jane sequence of stories—new to her fiction as well as to family-based fiction in general—is Gilchrist's attention to biological inheritance: the role of genetics in family heritage and personal expression and fulfillment.

Nora Jane's horror is, as we have learned, that Sandy will observe his own features in Lydia's and will immediately recognize her as his own child. Genetic connections cast both sunlight and shadow over the entire Nora Jane sequence; and these two aspects—spirituality in the form of love *and* a sense of scientific inevitability when it comes to the will of chromosomes—as well as the collection's major thematic framework of personal security and ensuring the security of loved ones, all converge beautifully and meaningfully together in the consciousness of Nieman, Freddy's best friend since boyhood, and himself a protector of Freddy's family. Nieman, in reflecting on his feelings for the Haywoods and, in the process, offering a summary of the spiritual and scientific underpinnings of the whole set of Nora Jane stories, says, "So what if they are not mine, not related to me. All life comes from one cell. They are mine because they have my heart."[31]

A discussion of these stories must include an identification of one particular—and particularly charming—symbol of security, safety, love, *and* the benefits of scientific knowledge that recurs in the series: an old brown cape. The cape first appears in "You Must Change Your Life," a story that verges on magic realism. Nieman is the story's protagonist, and it will be recalled from a previous story that he, along with Freddy, has returned to taking classes at Berkeley at the same time Nora Jane has enrolled as a beginning student. As this story opens, Nieman quits his very prestigious job as a newspaper film critic to jump full-tilt into the role of student. He intends to study all he can about science.

Nieman is visited in a dream by Leonardo da Vinci: an experience that only reinforces his sense, his conviction, that he has so much to learn and only a relatively short time in which to learn it. When Leonardo leaves the dream, he is simply gone like an apparition; but he leaves behind his brown cape. The next story is called "The Brown Cape," and from it comes the realization that the cape *actually* exists; and here the element of magic realism holds sway, of course, but reasonably and even beautifully so; the cape emanates from a dream, but it is left behind as an actual physical item, which Nieman insists he can't remember owning. In "The Brown Cape," Freddy and the twin girls take a hiking trip and Freddy ends up injured; and the cape, which the girls had found and stuck into a backpack, they now wrap around his injured limbs, and the three of them are rather miraculously rescued off the mountain. The cape resurfaces in two more stories and offers a delightful interconnection between them. In "The Affair," Nieman has found a girlfriend, Stella, about whom he gets serious very quickly. (This is not actually one of the stories in which the cape appears, but reading it is almost necessary so the remaining two capes stories make complete sense.) Stella isn't getting any younger; and, in keeping with the science motif running through these stories—more specifically, the scientific side of inheritance— Stella reminds herself that she "should use one of [her] eggs. No one else carries Grandfather Bass's genes. No one else carries Mother's or Aunt Georgia's."[32] Stella is a physicist and biochemist at the university, which is how she meets Nieman. She and he fall in love nearly at first sight. And this new distraction keeps Nieman from obsessing about his new quest for scientific knowledge. At story's end one of the twins says to her sister, "Uncle Nieman will never get a Nobel now. Dad says Nieman has forgotten all about wanting a Nobel prize for biochemistry."[33] It is difficult not to feel he is better off!

In the following story, "Design," the brown cape surfaces again, in a box of old clothes from the Salvation Army, delivered to a girls' orphanage. The little girl Gabriela takes the cape into her possession, for "something about it appealed to her. It reminded her of a lighter, warmer world . . . someplace that was warm and sunny. . . ."[34] Meanwhile a couple in Oklahoma has communicated a desire to adopt a little girl, and the orphanage proposes Gabriela; in the end not only Gabriela, but also her best friend Annie, gets adopted by this couple as well.

The next story, "A Wedding by the Sea," is the last of the cape sequence-within-a-sequence stories. Nieman and Stella are getting married, and Stella's cousin from Oklahoma is coming to the wedding, bringing the two girls she and her husband recently adopted, none other than Gabriela and Annie from the previous story. As it turns out, Gabriela had taken the cape with her to Oklahoma; and now, as a guarantee against their new parents dropping them back at the orphanage when they return to California, she again takes the cape with her. But Nora Jane's twins do not recognize it as the same cape they had found and used to help their father keep warm and dry during his hiking accident; the twins recognized it as just a cape that looks like the one they used to have. Nonetheless, it cements a new friendship between the two pairs of girls.

The remaining nine stories in the collection *The Courts of Love*—the stories falling outside the Nora Jane sequence, that is—actually share with the sequence its major thematic underpinning: personal security and safety for oneself and for one's loved ones. Surprisingly, ironically, but ultimately understandably, the first of these "outsider" stories is also one about Nora Jane; but with the sequence given the heading "Nora Jane and Company;" and this one—titled "New Orleans"—featuring Nora Jane as a little girl back in her hometown, it is rightly excluded. In fact, it is a companion piece to "The Blue House" in *The Age of Miracles*. Both stories indicate Nora Jane's early psychological and emotional fortitude in dealing with a drunken mother who is dysfunctional in raising Nora Jane; both stories are instructive in understanding the provenance of the adult Nora Jane's strength of character:

as preludes, then, to seeing the actions and effects of the mature Nora Jane in the "Nora Jane and Company" sequence.

Animals appear in this collection as characters in their own right (as opposed to ancillary "characters" as they were in the novel *Anabasis*): they are created not as cutesy, anthropomorphic creatures, but they are rendered in an empathetic, entirely dignified fashion, their states of mind sensitively entered into. In "Fort Smith," the animal character is a little black bear on his own, away from his mother for the first time ("The small bear was getting very unhappy. . . . There was food everywhere but he couldn't find it.")[35] A dog—obviously—is the pivotal character in the story "The Dog Who Delivered Papers to the Stars," which is one of the most poignant stories Gilchrist has ever written. One more time she demonstrates her ability to begin a story in an absolutely compelling fashion, to guarantee that the reader can not possibly resist continuing: "When Copey Culp's wife stole his children and went home to her people, the first thing he did was take her dog out in the woods and shoot it."[36]

The dog's name is Dan, and he is a golden retriever; and no reader who has an ounce of affection for animals can help but fall in love with Dan—love at first sight, that is. He is a wonderfully modest hero: like Freddy Harwood, Nora Jane's husband (both of them, in all *seriousness*, are two of the most sensitively drawn of Gilchrist's male "characters.") Dan had come to Harrisburg (the little southern Illinois town that is also the setting for some of the Rhoda-as-little-girl stories) "with a crew who came to town to shoot background scenes for a movie about Frank and Jesse James."[37] His owner insisted to Copey's wife, who was on the set with their little boys (extras in the film), that Dan "has delivered papers to the stars."[38] The boys immediately fall in love with Dan, and his owner let them keep him; and he stayed with Copey and his family for two years: until Copey's wife up and left him.

But even though Copey did indeed shoot Dan in retaliation, the dog survives—unbeknown to Copey, who left him for dead. Dan was taken by a passerby to the town animal shelter where, after surgery to repair the bullet damage, Dan recovers. In not too long a time, Dan is adopted by a young man who has come to town to die: he is an AIDS sufferer, and he has wanted to go to a small and quiet place where he was unknown and no one would ask questions. Dan and William establish a fast, deep bond; and even when Copey, who is threatened with bodily harm by his wife's brothers unless he ships her dog to her home in Kentucky, recognizes Dan with William, the dog is attached now to his beloved new owner. At night "Dan moved his big warm body closer to William's legs. He heard the earth's core and the blood coursing through William's veins and the distant call of a mourning dove. It was dark and warm in the room and he was safe. He closed his eyes and saw a line of newspapers on a sunny street. They were waiting for him. When he woke he would deliver them to their people."[39]

Without sentimentality coating this story as if it were dipped in sugar, Gilchrist has composed a deeply effecting variation on the collection's theme of survival: in this take on the theme, the mutuality of man and man's best friend together holding up against great physical odds. It is simply one of her most moving stories.

Gilchrist's next book is her last novel to date, published in 1997 and titled, in simple fashion for her (given her noted propensity for *complex* titles), *Sarah Conley*. It stands as Gilchrist's greatest achievement so far in the novel form; she has everything right in this one, able to focus all her tendency for concise, direct writing even over the expanded pages of a novel. This one takes readers to her usual milieu, the contemporary South, and she has carried over into it all the sense of rousing drama she exhibited in her ancient Greece novel, *Anabasis*. *Net of Jewels* was certainly a compelling exploration of the character of Rhoda, but in *Sarah Conley*, Gilchrist conceives of and executes the eponymous character as a stronger, less manipulative, and general more pleasant and sympathetic person than Rhoda Manning.

Sarah Conley is a novel about possibilities in life—specifically, about having the courage to face possibilities and gathering one's forces and resources to accept them, or at least to have good, sound reasons for rejecting them. It is therefore a novel about the need to come to decisions—however grudgingly—concerning which direction one's life ought to proceed. It is a novel about the transitions of middle age: accepting and learning from the first half of adult life and gauging whether the best approach to the second half is retrenchment, maintaining the status quo, or attempting to forge new avenues no matter how frightening such a prospect may be.

The time in which the novel is set is 1996, and Sarah Conley is in her early fifties. She lives in New York City, and she holds an editorial position at *Time* magazine. The novel actually opens with a flashback to Sarah's adolescence in her hometown of Tyler, Kentucky. Sarah's father has died, only a few months prior to when we step into the story; and her mother is obsessed with the possibility, however unlikely, of destitution. Sarah has secured an amazing job for a 14-year-old: writing a column for the local newspaper. On assignment to do a piece about the town's swimming pool, Sarah meets a new girl in town, Eugenie, whose father owns coalmines, and who is consequently not facing poverty by any means. Sarah is immediately impressed with Eugenie. She "had never met a girl who was so sure of herself."[40] Without feeling she was sponging, she lets Eugenie's father, over the years, pay for things for her—including, when the time comes, her tuition to Vanderbilt.

So as we return to the novel's real time, 1996, we see Sarah in her third year as a *Time* editor, a job about which she has ambivalence. (The pull to be "out in the field" being a writer rather than stuck in an office "putting out fires" and taking meetings about covers is the source of her distress over her position.)

She has a much-younger, live-in boyfriend, who, also a writer, isn't being repaid the rewards of success like he feels he should be; and his whining grates on Sarah. One day, in January of that year, Sarah receives a call at her office from the man who had married her dear friend Eugenie, to inform her Eugenie is dying. Upon hearing this devastatingly news, Sarah says, aloud but to herself, "We were strong and beautiful and brave and now the dying starts."[41]

At this point in the narrative, another flashback fills in more details about the history of Sarah and Eugenie's friendship; in nine pages, a wealth of information is given that explains the basis of what will happen throughout the rest of the novel. In this flashback, Sarah and her friend are both students at Vanderbilt; Eugenie has just met the man she is certain, from the outset, she will marry. His name is Jack McAllen; and when Sarah meets him, chemistry between *them*—between her and Jack—is palpable. Soon Sarah meets Jack's brother Timothy, younger, but also a Vanderbilt student. "Timothy was taller than Jack, less intense, more open and predictable and forgiving."[42] Soon the four of them are essentially inseparable. Around campus, "they became a legend, for their accomplishments, their gaiety, their united front."[43] Sarah accepted the chemistry between herself and Jack. "She was not yet to the point where guilt could make her sad or make her slow. If she knew that she and Jack had more in common that she and Timothy, it didn't matter. That was how it was. It was an imperfect world and all she knew for sure was that she was going to have her share of all these imperfections."[44]

But in the last month of their undergraduate period at Vanderbilt, something happened to change the nature of her relationship with Jack. Jack and Eugenie were formally engaged by this point, and these two, as well as Timothy, were slated to attend Vanderbilt medical school in the fall; and

Sarah had a job at the *Atlanta Constitution*. She and Timothy probably would become engaged soon, too. But Jack and Sarah give in to their mutual attraction and make love, after which they "held each other long enough so that it would never be over now, never, never, never."[45] Thus is established the frame upon which the course of this novel is stretched, to be sketched in with dramatic details: that which has been generated between Sarah and Jack by having committed sex would never be destroyed, never erode, but would always impose complications on their lives.

That very night Sarah also had sex with Timothy, this for the first time between the two of them as well, Sarah acting not so much out of a desire as out of realizing the necessity of instructing Jack and herself, futilely of course, that "we will forget [their sexual episode] ever happened."[46] Sarah soon discovers herself to be pregnant, and without the certain knowledge of the baby's true paternity—Jack's baby or Timothy's—she marries Timothy in a month's time. A month after that Jack and Eugenie are married; but Jack is nearly relentless in his insistence to Sarah that each of them has made a huge mistake in *not* marrying each other. Although Sarah recognizes the truth of Jack's sentiment, Timothy represents a stable future; whereas any future with Jack means only the betrayal of her beloved friend Eugenie and Eugenie's father, who, as will be recalled, footed the bill for Sarah's education.

But Sarah's marriage to Timothy lasted only six years—this information supplied in the crucially important flashback chapter—and then for five years she and Timothy dueled each other over custody of Jimmy, their child (or is he her and Jack's child?); and Sarah eventually looses the fight.

Sarah has her newspaper job in Atlanta; while employed there she writes a novel "to pay Timothy and Jennifer [his new wife] and Jack and Eugenie and Nashville back for what they had done."[47] The novel was nominated for a National Book Award and led to her job at *Time*, where she is currently employed—this, of course, in the novel's real time.

Another situation pertaining to Sarah and the people back home is also explained in this essential backstory chapter. Her friends and family, including her son Jimmy, are furious with her at what she exposed in her novel; and from that point to the present, to the day Jack calls to tell Sarah that Eugenie is quickly dying, there has been no communication between Sarah and the people she left behind in Nashville, with the slight exception of her son, with whom she remains in irregular contact. Because of this situation—because of Sarah's estrangement from Nashville—her return to attend Eugenie on her sick bed amounts to traveling to a foreign country. The country of her birth, but from which she emigrated early. And now *it* is the country that is for-eign. "You can't go home again" is a maxim tested to the fullest in this novel. After all that has happened, *can* Sarah go home again, not in the physical sense, of course, but in the psychological sense? In the sense of reconnection with people and recreating the roles she played back then while not down-playing the person she has become?

Eugenie dies within hours of Sarah's arrival at her bedside. Now, then, arises the major conflict that will define the novel, the serious conflict that will have to be addressed by Sarah; and the conflict is three-fold, a choice of three possibilities, each choice automatically excluding the other two. One, Jack, his wife now dead, lays his case before Sarah: to come back to live in Nashville and be his wife; and the fact that she has always loved him, and that he is a very successful physician, makes for great enticement. Two, con-tinue her life in New York as a *Time* editor, even though she is already bored with her work there, but of course this option provides steadiness and no surprises. Three, accept an offer that is being dangled before her to take a leave from *Time* to go to Paris to write a screenplay, a choice offering a great deal of money, which she could use for fixing up her grandparents' old farmhouse outside Nashville, a project she wants to embark on (since she's never had an actual home, having lived in apartments her adult life for 20 years) regardless of—outside from—any beckoning by Jack to return to Nashville.

Maintaining the status quo in New York or turning back to explore what was left behind at home in Nashville or jumping almost blindly into a new and risky but exciting adventure in Paris: Sarah most choose one. There is no way out of having to make a choice; these opportunities will not tolerate continued postponement. Understandably, though, Sarah wants them *not* to be mutually exclusive; she desires a combination of all of them: keep Jack loving her and wanting her back in Nashville, but not requiring her to be there full time; keep her job at *Time;* being allowed by her boss at *Time* to take a leave of absence to go to make some quick bucks in Paris. Complica-tions arise, of course. First of all, there are the children: Sarah's son Jimmy, who may or may not actually be Jack's son, and from whom Sarah has been quasi-estranged; and Jack's daughter, Elise, who is a walking definition of a dysfunctional personality. What would their reaction be to a marriage between Sarah and Jack? And, besides, Jimmy and Elise are involved in a destructive relationship themselves: bad enough for being the first cousins they believe themselves to be, but horrible given that they may actually be half-siblings (a fact unknown to them, of course, but information of which Sarah and Jack are only too aware).

Then there is Sarah's young live-in boyfriend to deal with. Sarah has grown tired of his "youngness": that which, in her eyes, was his greatest initial appeal is by now his biggest drawback.

So weeks pass, and Sarah puts off making a decision about her future with Jack or about traveling to Paris for a few weeks and writing a movie script there. In the meantime she is having her farmhouse back in Tennessee completely renovated, the work being designed and executed by Jack's daughter, Elise, who is an architect. Sarah "toys" with the house, insisting she may never live there in its rehabilitated comfort and attractiveness, but only rent it out, but at the same time, almost without recognizing the situation for what it really is, grasping onto the house, as if actually holding it in her hand, as a symbol of security amid the sea of irresolution that her life has become. The farmhouse is her family heritage. While Jack, her life and job in New York, and the chance to do the film script in Paris are three separate, almost water-tight compartments representing whole, entire, intact divisions of her life into past, present, and future, the farmhouse alone is the comforting connection running through all three otherwise seemingly mutually exclusive arenas, the one very concrete connection that keeps past, present, and future from flying off in different directions.

This brief exchange between Sarah and her agent shows not only the attachment to that property poignantly emphasized, but also Gilchrist's cogent use of dialogue:

"My father died on that farm. In the fields, hunting quail with his dogs. I was thirteen."

"You've never written about that."

"I know. I might now."

"Dangerous waters. See your analyst before you wade out into that."[48]

Events, as they turn out, happen quickly. Sarah agrees to marry Jack at some point, but not now. Elise completes rehabbing and refurbishing the farmhouse, but she succumbs to her private demons and kills herself after making the disastrous choice to have herself sterilized. Jimmy finds a woman to love and marries her, to Sarah's pleasure. Sarah's New York boyfriend goes to California to make it big. Sarah does indeed go to Paris and writes a screenplay the producers are happy with, taking a leave from *Time* that turns into a permanent termination from employment there when her boss, who had promised to keep her position open and let her have it again upon her return to New York, is fired in an office coup while Sarah is abroad. Finally, Jack grows too tired of waiting for Sarah and contracts a mutual understanding with a much younger nurse at the hospital where he works (a situation that lasts only a short while).

Resolution of Sarah's plight is perfectly satisfying while at the same time not artificially tidy. The last chapter, a little more than a page in length, offers a conclusion not only workable but pleasing—but not to be given away here.

Sarah Conley is a romantic but honest, wise, and certainly beautiful novel. Romantic in the sense that it deals with love and the anguish that love engenders, but rendered without being cloying or melodramatic. The novel's honesty lies in its rigorously authentic depiction of a strong, middle-aged, and successful female character. It can be called a wise novel because Gilchrist's characterizations could only have been created from great accumulation of knowledge about people gathered from years of keen-eyed, sympathetic, and empathetic observation of the human race. Such as when Eugenie dies, Sarah reflects to Jack, "I don't know how we are supposed to do anything. We are so brave, all us people of the earth, knowing we will die and not thinking of it all day every day. Then one of us does die and there we are faced with it, loss without end, loss that cannot be reversed. Our own loss coming."[49]

It is a beautiful novel, too, because Gilchrist's concise yet supple and fluid prose style is in full shine; for example, this passage as she describes the tension between Sarah and Jack the first time they were physically intimate: "It was very sexual, very tight, the moment strung like a violin."[50] Or when they encounter each other when Sarah returns to Nashville to see the dying Eugenie one last time: "Through all those barriers and all those years his touch had traveled."[51]

Contrary to my opinion of the novel, there was indeed critical negativity lobbed at it. The *New York Times* said it this way: "Almost from the beginning, melodramatic scenes and characters fail to win the novel credibility. And a chatty style heavy with extraneous detail feels like a way of avoiding a deeper exploration of the story's implications."[52] And *Booklist* insisted the plot was "hackneyed" and that, "instead of psychology, social commentary, or reflections on the human spirit, we get a tallying of items such as designer clothes, luxury automobiles, expensive jewels, and extravagant homes."[53] Upon later reflection, Margaret Donavan Bauer, in her book-length study of Gilchrist's fiction, posited "Although most of the novel develops the conflict involved when two career-oriented people try to make a life together, still there is little tension, little of the angst involved in deciding whether to compromise one's career goals for love, and all eventually winds up happily. . . ."[54]

Chapter 9

Even More Story Collections
(*Flights of Angels, The Cabal and Other Stories*)

SO FAR GILCHRIST HAS NOT WRITTEN ANOTHER NOVEL after *Sarah Conley*. The four books since its publication have been short story collections, the first of these being *Flights of Angels*, published in 1998. This collection gathers 19 stories, the collection as a whole not first-rate by the standards Gilchrist has set for herself in prior collections. With the exception of two stories narrated by Traceleen, the black maid of rich, bossy, and feisty Crystal Manning of New Orleans, both of whom are characters encountered on numerous previous occasions and always enjoyable to read about—with the exception of these two excellent stories, no bright lights emanate from this collection. In fact the three stories included here about the most recurrent of Gilchrist's characters, Rhoda Manning, are slight, not advancing the Rhoda character nor enhancing a reader's appreciation of her.

However, the collection *Flights of Angels* does serve to remind, particularly after the seriousness—but the *appropriate* seriousness—of the novel *Sarah Conley* and even after the brilliant but actually less-than-knee-slappingly funny short story collection just before this one, *The Courts of Love*, of Gilchrist's marvelous sense of humor. This quality is especially evident in the two Traceleen stories and particularly in the first, "Miss Crystal Confronts the Past," which delivers readers quickly back to the marvelously adventuresome world of Traceleen and her boss Crystal. Of course following Traceleen as she goes through the adventures that Crystal is such an expert at setting up is the sum and substance and pleasure of the Traceleen stories—

these forming the most entertaining category of all of Gilchrist's fiction. (Traceleen's role as recorder and narrator of these escapades is well expressed thus: "I know it is mean to gossip and tell tales. I don't know what comes over me and makes me do it. Still, somebody has to make a record. . . . All I am writing down is the things that change our lives. The things that seem almost to happen of their own accord, as if a big mist falls over the land and puts ideas into our heads."[1] Delicious disingenuousness.)

Money is at the bottom of the adventure unfolding in "Miss Crystal Confronts the Past"—specifically, Crystal's brother, Phelan, whom we have met before, is squandering the family fortune on gambling and supporting a slew of ex-wives. As the story opens, Phelan is visiting his and Crystal's grandmother in Charlotte, North Carolina, and Crystal has gone there from New Orleans, with Traceleen in tow, to attempt to interfere in some fashion with the likelihood that Phelan, who apparently is planning to spend a whole year with their grandmother in her house, keeping her well amused and entertained, will siphon off all the inheritance, leaving Crystal to, in the end, inherit nothing from the intimidating old lady. Their grandmother may be old, but she retains the grit and spunk that have always made her a formidable player in family members' business. Attempting to stand between her forceful grandmother and her weak but manipulating brother, Crystal is, as Traceleen observes, "thrown back into her powerless position in a family that favors males."[2] Indeed, Phelan is the oldest grandson, "a position of great and awesome power and the power runs both ways. The paternal grandmother and the oldest grandson have a river of power that runs between them like a torrent that never stops."[3] In Crystal's estimation, this river of power flows completely *around* her, leaving her high and dry. Nor does it go unnoticed by the chronically, habitually *noticing* Traceleen that when Phelan attends to his grandmother, she glows. How is Crystal to compete with that? Not easily, to be sure. Traceleen admits that Crystal's part of the inheritance is now truly threatened.

Shortly after Traceleen and Crystal arrive at Crystal's grandmother's house, Phelan decides the old woman needs an upgrade in her sound system, so she could listen to her favorite opera singers; going shopping, he whisks Crystal off with him. Traceleen learns the details of the shopping expedition later from Crystal, and Traceleen's marvelously droll way of narrating events, and even events she is not privy to, is just plain funny here. It seems that Phelan and Crystal first go to an electronics store, Phelan finding "the only woman salesperson and [he] put some moves on her and gave her his phone number and then picked out a three-hundred dollar CD player and speakers and paid for it with cash."[4] Then off to a record store, and Phelan "found the youngest woman salesperson and did some moves on her and gave her his phone number and then bought a hundred dollars' worth of CDs."[5]

When Crystal broaches the subject of their grandmother's finances to him, specifically whether the old lady has enough to support herself in her declining years, Phelan brushes her off with the insistence that, with Medicare and Social Security and the property she owns, she is fine. Crystal is not to worry. As it turns out, Phelan is scamming Medicare; and although Crystal couldn't prove it, Phelan's scam was making their grandmother a fortune—which the old lady knew about. Afraid of their potential status as accessories to the crime, Crystal and Traceleen hightail it out of town and go back home to New Orleans. The grandmother dies the following fall, and Phelan goes off to Europe; and he is across the ocean when officials begin looking into his Medicare record keeping. "It was a good living,"[6] Traceleen concludes, after she and Crystal calculate how much Phelan probably earned for himself and their grandmother. But Crystal's husband Manny insists the whole thing is Crystal's imagining. Upon hearing this response, Traceleen is undoubtedly shaking her head as she posits, "I will never understand the male psyche. They are running a different course than we women are, they are sailing different seas, they dance to different tunes."[7]

So, Traceleen has set herself up to be the recorder of deeds: the deeds that comprise the never-a-dull-moment life of her boss, Crystal Manning. Traceleen's take on Manning family matters, on the human condition in all its frailties and posturing, but also in its moments of strength as practiced and epitomized by the Manning family, is rendered in the best kind of humor: holding up the ridiculousness of family behavior to public view, but the arched eyebrow of her who is doing the holding up is arched not out of disdain, and certainly not out of contempt, but out of an appreciation of or at least a resignation to the fact that none of us is immune from being ridiculous at some point or other.

A second interesting aspect of the collection *Flights of Angels*, in addition to its display of humor, is Gilchrist's tackling of social issues that extend past the confines of family matters; these are national issues, important problems in American life at the end of the twentieth century, especially in southern American life. Gilchrist is consistent in her interest in a character's *personal* past: how one's earlier life and family history determine or at least influence present and probable future attitudes and behavior. Now, in some stories in this particular collection, she casts characters' personal and familial pasts, as well as their current behavioral patterns, against a strongly textured backdrop of contemporary social problems, particularly how the ways of the Old South conflict with the more modern ways of the New South.

A case in point is "Mississippi." The major issue into which this story delves, the issue explored here loftier than any individual's life and family past and personal pursuits, is the civil rights movement, which provoked a particularly painful transition in customs and politics in Gilchrist's native state. The story opens—Gilchrist's talent for grabbing the reader almost without time to take a breath once again in evidence—with a face-slapping urgency: "She sat in her cell awaiting her death. Death was imminent. They had done it, they had been caught, tried, and convicted, and unless the governor of Mississippi called in the next two hours they were going to be put to death."[8]

The necessary seriousness for such a sociologically oriented story is quickly made obvious. Larkin is the name of the primary character, and she has the time and need to think about, while sitting on the hard bed in her cell, how she grew up with privilege in the Delta. She knew Someral, who is black, since childhood. In a demonstration in Jackson, Someral, now a student at Millsaps College, was killed—intentionally—by a hit-and-run driver; and Larkin, who was present and a witness, recognized the man behind the wheel. But the man Larkin identified to the authorities went unquestioned, so she and two of her male friends went to find him, and they shot and killed him. Despite incarceration and probably execution, Larkin experiences no remorse: "How much she had loved killing him and did not regret it."[9]

What she does regret is that Someral had not wanted to be at the demonstration in the first place. He had his education (so vastly important to him and his family) and the pleasure of going out on archaeological digs to think about, to occupy his time and thoughts, not going on marches. But Larkin got him to participate in this one. "I egged him on to do it," she recalls. "So here he came, in his little crooked glasses and his skinny arms and legs and bookworm smile and he stood out in the crowd. He stood out anywhere he went. So maybe Jacob [the hit-and-run driver] took him for a Yankee. I wish I could have asked him that before I shot him."[10]

In form, this story is essentially a flashback to past events and people in Larkin's life as she awaits the governor's decision whether to commute her death sentence. And the crux of the story, the "heart" of it, the significance and resonance of it, comes to the fore when Larkin thinks back on her grandfather and his influence on her. What she feels about the impact of Granddaddy on the way she was to shape her own life now informs her how she came to be sitting in this prison cell facing death sanctioned by the state; and in these moments of Larkin's reflection, Gilchrist achieves poignancy by way of absolute beauty of prose. "Granddaddy never let the black people be left out of anything because he helped them and he loved them," Larkin recalls, and thus reasons, "It's Granddaddy's fault I'm going to die. . . . [I]t's Granddaddy's fault . . . for teaching us to respect all men and Momma and Daddy's for dying when I was five years old and leaving us to be raised by old people who read Greek at night and didn't believe in hating anyone."[11]

Gilchrist persists in her problematic point of view shifts in her stories—sometimes actually adding to the narrative's effectiveness, enriching its impact; but at other times her habit is detrimental to the story, sidetracking the reader and dulling the story's sharpness. In this story as well, Gilchrist does nothing to abandon her tendency; but this occasion proves to be one of the times when it works to the story's advantage. Specifically, the point of view shifts from Larkin to Jacob Miley, the young man who used his car to murder Larkin's friend Someral and who, in turn, would be shot and killed by Larkin herself. His backstory is told, and, as well as holding the reader's interest, Gilchrist artfully uses Jacob's biography (an abbreviation of it, of course) and mental state for larger purposes than to simply impart a taste of him. For he and his narrow racist views stand for the mentality against which the civil rights movement had to push. The artful aspect of his employ by Gilchrist is that she makes him more than just a type, makes him, in amazingly brief space, a very personal figure, making him distinctive and real and drawing him into the story, not simply as some abstract form passing into the frame for ill-defined or convenient reasons.

Larkin had met Jacob the year before, had a one-night stand with him—and a heated discussion about integration. Only minutes after sex, she regretted it, wondering to herself "what had made her fuck a racist midget."[12]

Toward the story's end another point of view shift occurs, with mixed effect this time. It is brief but jarring; it does, however, explain how and why the story will end as it does. We are witness to the governor of Mississippi as he listens to "his crazy daughter," who, as it turns out, "had gone to camp with Larkin Flowers. Larkin had been nice to her when no one else at the camp liked her. Larkin was a heroine to Wilma Marie. She couldn't believe her daddy was going to let Larkin die."[13] And indeed he does *not* let her die.

Larkin could, if she so desired, take heart from the reprieve that the goodness that goes around comes around, and use the power of that first-hand knowledge to help her cope with her feelings of guilt about Someral's death. But she doesn't, at least not in the first few minutes of learning of the governor's pardon; she just cries over all the badness in the world: an almost uncomfortable yet tenable, even satisfying, ending to a story in which Gilchrist extends herself, with sure-footedness, into the realm of political fiction and out of her typical domestic and familial arenas, doing so with finesse—no preachiness, no message-sending of the sort that can turn fiction into tract.

Her next book, *The Cabal and Other Stories,* published in 2000, closely on the heels of her previous book, is—obviously from the title—another compilation of short fiction. This particular collection features a novella—the title piece—and five stories. Gilchrist has not extensively explored the novella form; before this, she had written only the three novellas gathered in *I Cannot Get You Close Enough,* only one of those proving very effective—but the lack of effectiveness in the other two stemming from their weakness of subject matter rather than from any clumsiness with the form itself. In fact, as Gilchrist did indeed show in the third of the three novellas in that collection ("A Summer in Maine") and now shows in the novella in this collection, she enjoys a comfort with letting the narrative go longer and more elaborately developed—adding more detail and deeper value to the sketching of her characters but, at the same time, erecting a tighter structure, as the form dictates, than she would in a novel.

The initial reaction to this collection is its flatness. No story suggests itself as one to be listed among the best she has written (although one story comes close, and it will be discussed later in terms of its effectiveness and superiority within the collection). But the material is simply mediocre, then? That is not the case; it is, in fact, an excellent collection. The problem is, it is *consistently* good; the problem is, following Gilchrist's career from start to finish like this, an increasing number of high-quality, even breathtaking, stories is easy to come to be expected from her; yet this gathering does not soar above what has come before it. Is the conclusion to be drawn, then, that she has not taken steps forward—and upward?

Not in the least. It is just that this particular collection suffers from its "context": essentially, that it is another of Gilchrist's excellent story collections, not superior to the others, but certainly *as* superior. Consequently, perhaps the more telling or at least more helpful way to react to *The Cabal and Other Stories* is viewing it as someone new to Gilchrist would see it—a reader unfamiliar with the "context."

"The Cabal," as previously indicated, is a novella. Its 130 pages fill half the book. It is set in Jackson, Mississippi, and the first sentence of the "Preface" sets the stage: "This is the story of a group of people who had a bizarre and unexpected thing happen to them." Then the situation at hand is broadened with "The psychiatrist went crazy and started injecting himself with drugs. The most useful and dependable man in their lives became a maniac in the true sense of the word. He was the glue that held their group together. He was the one who had taught them to trust one another. He had told each one of them the best things he knew about the others. One by one he planted seeds of kindness and empathy in their hearts."[14]

His name is Jim Jaspers, and "later, when he went mad, [his clients] didn't know what to do. It tore the fabric of their common reality. A brilliant, useful man who had spent his days solving other people's problems became the cause of them. Much harm was done, many sleepless nights were spent by the twenty-two people [who, as we soon come to learn, are the cabal of the title] who had put their lives in his hands."[15]

The Preface cogently lays out the plan of the narrative to come: "This is the story of some of them."[16] The 14 sections and a "postscript" follow the trauma in the lives of these people as presented by their therapist not only putting himself out of commission—out of their reach to continue giving them emotional life-support—but also threatening an even more calamitous situation: revealing his clients' confidentialities to one another. The latter would be, of course, a matter of concern for anyone consulting a therapist; but doubly troubling in a close-knit society such as the so-called cabal, for whom image is everything, and any image besmirchment spells absolute disaster. The cabal offers itself only too readily as a laboratory for Gilchrist to explore and experiment with her acute sense of social satire; and this novella, then, becomes a delectable comic parable of contemporary upper-middle-class social life. This group of artistic and socially well-placed individuals in Jackson, Mississippi, is a perfect vehicle for her to deliver stiletto-sharp jabs at the now socially acceptable—no, socially *mandatory*—exercise of turning to therapy as a necessity for coping with life's problems and learning if one's special quirks are too outlandish for social acceptability. Over the heads of members of the closed community of the cabal, all of whom know each other as clients of this same therapist, Jim Jaspers, hangs the prospect of instant mortification if not only their foibles but also their secrets are exposed to public scrutiny. For Gilchrist, and consequently for her readers, it is simply too delicious to resist.

Light on the inner workings of the cabal is provided by a "worm" boring into its interior, and the worm is Caroline Jones, introduced as she is driving at top speed to Mississippi. In the novella's opening two paragraphs, the nature of her mission becomes clear: She is heading to Jackson from Nashville, where she had been living with her parents in a rather forced retreat after being taken in a scam to write for the movies in Hollywood, for which she had ruinously quit her teaching post at Yale. It is Thursday as the story opens; Caroline needs to be in Jackson by the following Monday morning to fill in for a writing teacher at Millsaps College, who had died unexpectedly the week before. This opportunity is affording Caroline a double benefit: work, which she needs, and also "a chance to regain her status in academia."[17]

Not to reduce this narrative to the level of television comedies, but Caroline functions for the reader like the character of Marilyn in the classic 1960s television show *The Munsters* did for the viewing audience. Both are the "normal" person from the outside who comes to live on the inside. Through Caroline, as through Marilyn in the TV show, through the contrast these two characters establish while on the inside, as well as by way of their instant rapport with the "inmates" that coincides with their continued footing in the real world outside the hermetically sealed environment of weirdness into which they have stepped, the reader, who is also on the outside, is brought in and allowed to look over Caroline's shoulder, as over Marilyn's shoulder in *The Munsters,* as she reacts and adjusts to these people's idiosyncrasies—to which she herself remains sympathetic, but at the same time she performs as a central intelligence through which the reader constantly processes the fact that what these people exhibit are *indeed* idiosyncrasies that are if not engendered at least exaggerated by the closedness of their social environment.

Caroline had heard about the job opening through an old friend who teaches there at Millsaps, good-looking Augustus Hailey, who had been her best friend at Vanderbilt. Augustus's telephone call had informed her, as an extra pitch to come to Jackson to live and teach, that the town has a theater group. "The people who run this town are in it."[18] It is he who refers to them as a cabal, and he proceeds to explain that all the cabal members go to the same therapist. "Isn't that a kick?" he remarks to Caroline. "On Monday morning he gets to hear six different versions of the cast party from the weekend before."[19]

Caroline arrives in Jackson to be met with consequential news—which sets off the chain reaction that is the *materiel* of the novella. She must hurry and get changed, for Augustus is taking her to a funeral right away; the rich and powerful Jean Lyles, the founder of this local theater group Augustus had talked about, died at age sixty, quite suddenly, leaving a family of grown-up sons and a lover of 29! The funeral turns out to be a power play between the family on one side and the lover and his supporters on the other; the sons are in the process of kicking the lover, Mack Stanford by name, out of the late Jean's house. Caroline thoroughly enjoys herself. "It was already the best funeral she had ever attended."[20]

At the post-funeral reception, things take an even more dramatic turn. Jim Jaspers, the therapist to whom everyone in the cabal goes, loses control and starts acting out in a crazy fashion, taking off his clothes. Eventually he storms off, but not before throwing some private matters into the faces of some of the attendees—his clients—in front of everyone else.

Later at the event, Caroline is introduced to Celia Montgomery, married to a very rich man and one of the founding members of the cabal; and Celia immediately requests a favor of Caroline. Celia's daughter, CeCe, attends Millsaps and aspires to be a writer, and could Caroline sort of take CeCe under her wing? Caroline is now suspicious of Augustus's request that she come to Millsaps to fill in as a writing teacher. Was she brought here simply to be caretaker of rich and mighty (and Millsaps board member) Celia's "wayward child"?

Over the next few days, the question on the cabal's collective mind is, "Did he [Jim Jaspers] say anything about me?"[21] The irony of their obsession with how much Jim has snitched on his clients is that it is almost a personal badge of honor if he *has* divulged personal information. As in any social group in which appearance is everything, every little movement or reaction is interpreted as an indicator of the possible shift in someone else's position in the pecking order, and, in this case, it is almost a sign of how important one is *if* Jim Jaspers is telling tales out of school about you. Caroline is not so much perceiving the irony of this herself as she is letting readers realize it for themselves as they peer over her shoulder to observe her not necessarily *in*voluntarily involvement in this spreading mess. Caroline is a published poet—her excellent volume of poetry is generally what got her this new teaching job—so all this drama going on around her is only grist for her writerly mill.

When Caroline reports to work, she has to hear the head of the English department—her new boss, in other words—encourage her to talk to CeCe, the daughter of big and important Celia Montgomery, whom Caroline has just met; it is a project Caroline was not too happy to assume. "A squeeze play, Caroline decided. I'll be damned."[22] When Caroline first meets the writing seminar, "It would have been hard to miss CeCe Montgomery. Even in a group of students with the moxie to think they could be writers she stood out. . . . The thought of counseling CeCe about anything seemed impossible. She was as hard-looking as an iron cube."[23]

Caroline is invited to Celia's Delta plantation the following weekend, a house party that will include Caroline's good friend Augustus, CeCe, and Mack Standford, the young lover of the recently deceased theater manager, Jean Lyles. Caroline is quite smitten with Mack. "He's the sexiest man I've ever seen in my life. I just want to warm my hands at that fire."[24] Caroline's eye for the handsome male far overrides every other concern. She rationalizes not only her attraction to Mack but also her whole participation in the cabal's business in this fashion: On her way to the house party in the Delta, she is "believing she had money and power figured out and in their place. . . . She felt no envy for Celia's money or her airplane. All she felt was curiosity about these new people who were making their way into her life. Of course, there was Mack Stanford. What he had was way past money or the trashy power it buys. He had the real thing. Real sexuality and kindness and charisma."[25]

The weekend at the Delta plantation proves quite cataclysmic. In the first place, once Caroline is under the roof of Celia's magnificent house, she decides she loves the rich. "This is okay. This is fine with me."[26] But, more importantly, word comes to the plantation that the deranged Jim Jaspers is on his way. Celia attempts to draw up a battle plan, for "he's running around the state of Mississippi like a loose shotgun."[27] But Jim kills himself in a car crash en route.

In spite of the turmoil swirling around them, Caroline and CeCe have a chance to exchange some meaningful words. Caroline, in both a plea and admonition, admits to CeCe that she believed her mother's request that Caroline make friends with CeCe was conspiracy, and admits to hating being used, but ultimately admits, too, that CeCe's smile now makes her want to be CeCe's friend.

So Caroline might be a little dazzled by the wealth into which she had stepped and made a little dizzy by the beauty of Mack Stanford, but she demonstrates that she has her head on straight when it comes to dealing with and accepting the obvious ticket that will ensure her overall success in this teaching venture at Millsaps College: CeCe, daughter of the mover and shaker Caroline Montgomery.

But another unexpected event is about to happen. In what we have seen to be traditional Gilchrist fashion, what better way to stir things up—stirring up the mind-set of her female protagonists, that is—than by introducing a new handsome man into the mix? In this case, a doctor from Memphis, and a good friend of Celia's, comes down to the Delta to try to settle people's craziness over Jim Jasper's *actual* craziness. His name is Royals Connell. He is quite handsome, and nothing has sprung into place between Caroline and Mack, the young lover of the newly deceased Jean Lyles, much against Caroline's plan, of course; since nothing has begun there, Caroline is only too happy to look Royals in the eye, note his attractiveness, and slip into his bed.

They—the cabal—decide to have Jim's cremation and funeral service there in the Delta, for "these were theater people. They know how to create an atmosphere."[28] The story is wrapped up in four final paragraphs, which are information packed and even face slapping in their abrupt summation of events. It is learned that Caroline and Royals conceived twin babies during that weekend in the Delta; they married and Caroline gives up her teaching position at Millsaps to move to Memphis and be a wife and mother. Out of death, so Gilchrist gives reassurance, life rises Phoenix-like to provide a succeeding generation. The ending connects the novella with the cosmos, connecting its particular details with *the* inexorable pattern of all patterns: life and death. But then the last page is turned to see that, as Gilchrist began the novella with a preface, she ends it with a postscript, which carries the storyline even farther along in time. From it is learned that Caroline's student, CeCe Montgomery, whom Caroline at first believed she needed to resent because she thought she had been brought to Millsaps to play babysitter to, but quickly during the course of the Delta weekend came to like and enjoy; it is learned that in the meantime CeCe has written a novel based on Jim Jaspers and the cabal. She takes the manuscript to Memphis to have it read by Caroline, whose response is lukewarm at best. This more writerly ending, based on the premise that life is reflected in art, that *from* life and its most mundane or outrageous manifestations comes art, is connected to the more universal, more cosmic pre-postscript ending by, in the postscript, CeCe's reactions to Caroline's four-month-old twins. At first CeCe finds them tiresome, but especially when she discovers "how fabulously sweet they smelled,"[29] maternal buttons are pushed. In the final paragraph, we learn that CeCe's manuscript went untouched after the encounter with Caroline and her babies—the implication being left in the air that CeCe went off to be creative in another direction, contributing to that greatest of cycles, birth, death, and renewal.

Gilchrist riffs on the death-and-birth theme in the five stories that accompany the novella. In fact, the first one to follow it, "The Sanguine Blood of Men," is actually a prequel to the novella itself. Caroline is the featured character again, but at a point in time before she came to Jackson to teach at Millsaps College. It will be recalled from the novella that Caroline quit her teaching position at Yale to go write for the movies, which was not a successful move for her, and she'd been forced to return to live with her parents in Nashville (from which she had been plucked by her friend Augustus to teach at Millsaps). This story, then, is about her final days in California writing for the movies; she is staying with her cousin LeLe Arnold in San Francisco. LeLe is a newspaper reporter and has a successful life; however, she hates being alone and is not happy that Caroline is planning to go back East. LeLe and Caroline are very close; Caroline believes her cousin to be "the most interesting, fascinating, and divine creature in the world."[30] But, still, Caroline is owed money by a studio and the whole movie-writing venture has definitely soured for her; and her last pitch to get the money owed her is a funny scene but, of course, not at all amusing to Caroline, until she views it as a victory in terms of the fact that the studio head "had made a pass at me"[31] and she had fielded it like a pro. That at least brings a smile to her face. And even though she is still planning to leave California, she has reconciled herself to the time spent there: an example of life's "opportunities and possibilities and surprises and irritations and danger."[32]

Anyway, that evening Caroline and LeLe must fly to Nashville, for their beloved grandmother has taken seriously ill and is dying. Upon their arrival at her beside, their grandmother dies—obviously waiting to take her last breath until her granddaughters can be with her. Caroline and LeLe fly back to California the day after the funeral, but Caroline only to pack up her car and turn around and leave again. Gilchrist's southern sensibilities—that identity with place so common thematically in southern literature, to which Gilchrist is not immune—come to the fore when Caroline informs her cousin, "I have a life if I'll go find it and it has to happen in the South . . . . I'm going home to where someone knows John Crowe Ransom and William Faulkner and James Baldwin."[33] This is not an indication of narrowness on Caroline's part; indeed, it is an aspect of, a manifestation in clear, bold language, of Gilchrist's realism in creating characters. When a venture does not work, especially one as life-altering as moving to a new place and taking a new job, it is only natural to want to return to one's home and familiar territory.

The difference between the short piece featuring the character of Caroline and the novella preceding it, in which, of course, she also featured as chief protagonist, is not simply length; the more meaningful difference is in tone and intent. "The Cabal," as we observed, and observed deliciously, is a sharply penetrating social satire: a comedy of manners. The story "The Sanguine Blood of Men," while richly veined with Gilchrist's trademark humor, is ultimately a more serious piece: a character study, rather than a dissection of social pretensions. The Caroline of the story is a pure example of the traditional Gilchrist female protagonist: strong, independent, self-respecting, and best in answering to her own needs and restorative environment. Caroline's return to her native South is not a retreat, not an escape. Her grandmother, whom she loved dearly, has died, and died in the South; and Caroline, ever so happy to be returning to the South, is by coming home in essence taking her grandmother's place—not in terms of place in the family, of course, but as a replacement from a succeeding generation of southern women.

"Hearts of Dixie" is also a prequel to "The Cabal." It is a first-person narrative told by the assistant to Jean Lyles, whose surprising death at the beginning of the novella set off the bizarre chain of events into which Caroline stepped into the middle of upon coming to Jackson to teach. It will be recalled that Jean Lyles was the director of the theater in Jackson; but Caroline does not feature in this story, which is about Jean's safe-deposit box that she had in her assistant's name; the assistant assumes the contents are her own to deal with upon Jean's untimely death. The contents include a cache of gold Krugerrands. Unfortunately this story is tiresome compared to its neighbors in the collection. It has little to say on the birth-replaces-death theme that binds the rest of the collection.

An ordinary but happy working wife in Fayetteville, Arkansas, makes the decision to go ahead and have an unplanned fourth child, a plan her very loving husband supports. This is the gist of the heartwarming but not sentimental "The Survival of the Fittest." But the beautiful "Bare Ruined Choirs, Where Late the Sweet Birds Sang" is arguably the best of the shorter pieces in the collection. The opening line is characteristically attention-grabbing, reader-ensnaring: "Dakota had decided to stop being selfish and go down to the coast and mix it up with her family."[34] The first paragraph goes on to explain that Dakota McAfee (a new, not recurrent, character) has several sons and daughters-in-law (current *and* ex) and two former husbands living on the Gulf Coast. Dakota has come to realize that "just because she was full of free-floating anxiety and had to clear up everything in the world didn't mean she had to foist her neuroses onto her progeny."[35] Every sentence in this story is wrought with sheer eloquence like this, rich in humor and in keenly understood and expressed truths about human nature.

Dakota owns a dress shop in Kansas City, Kansas (new character and *new locale* for Gilchrist), which has become quite successful for her, and it is difficult to pull herself away for just a couple of weeks for even something as important as visiting her family. As it turns out, Dakota has a little home in Ocean Springs, Mississippi, and there she actually will be staying while on this two-week "spiritual discipline,"[36] as she refers to it to a friend before leaving Kansas—as opposed to its simply being a vacation. As her mantra, Dakota repeats to herself, particularly as she faces meeting a brand new German daughter-in-law, "Let there be peace on earth and let it begin with me."[37] What Dakota doesn't know as she sets out on her long drive from Kansas to Mississippi is that her beloved great-aunt is dying; from her cousin, who lives in Memphis and whom Dakota calls from the road to ask to spend the night on her way down to the coast, she informed of this sad news. Consequently, Dakota stops in Memphis only long enough to pick up her cousin, and the two women head to the little Mississippi town where the old lady lies on her death-bed, and where Dakota has spent many summers when growing up.

Their arrival in town, to their great-aunt/grandmother's bedside, has a positive effect: "The room filled with light and laughter and people talking. Old death skulked out to the back hall and took a seat by the unused butter churn. This was not going to be his night after all. Two many lively, living people had come crawling in and taken the field."[38]

Of course, the whole episode of helping to tend to her dying relative functions to remind Dakota of not only her comfortable familial past and the excitement of being around men when you're still young and haven't hardened to romance; but it also prepares her better in the event of difficulties or at least discomfort in encountering all her children and their spouses, because in returning to the little Mississippi town where her great-aunt lived, for the first time in a long time, she re-encounters a man, a neighbor of her great-aunt's, who had been quite smitten with her one summer long ago. This man, George, accompanies Dakota to the Gulf Coast to see her family.

So, George—or, more specifically, the thrilling possibility of something good and meaningful arising between herself and him—is the perfect, perfectly healthy, distraction to keep Dakota from obsessing about getting along with family members, especially, her new daughter-in-law. With George she has new matters to occupy her mind. "They didn't need me,"[39] she realizes with no trace of bitterness, hurt, or even frustration—simply expressing an acceptance of the reality.

Of the shorter pieces in the collection, this story is the most poignant and resonant treatment of the abiding and binding theme of in life there is death but also renewal. Gilchrist takes a major step in her depiction of strong female characters here. Yes, Dakota needs a man, as all Gilchrist's independent women eventually do, despite protests and even actions to the contrary; but here her female protagonist finds a man, but not at the expense of family relations—which often happens in Gilchrist terrain. No, Dakota finding something in her old friend George simply strengthens her relations with her children by acknowledging they no longer need her and allowing feelings between herself and them to develop in the unforced way. In this delightful story, Gilchrist's voice rings loud and deep; it is a voice raised in song, in *celebration* of life—which gives it its consummate beauty.

The last story in the collection, "The Big Cleanup," is a yarn told by Traceleen, the black maid and best friend of rich Crystal Manning of New Orleans. Previous experience informs the reader, of course, that a Traceleen story is a pleasure—an expectation upheld here to only a modest degree. This particular Traceleen story is a visit to personal times past, a voyage into memory prompted by Crystal and Traceleen cleaning out all the drawers in Crystal's house. Her son, King, it will be remembered, is now married to Jessie Hand, niece of Anna Hand the famous writer now deceased, and King and Jessie live with their children in Atlanta; Crystal's daughter Crystal Anne is currently in college. Crystal is obviously suffering from the empty-nest syndrome, and her condition has rubbed off on Traceleen, too—relatively, to be sure, for as she declared to Crystal, "There's nothing to be learned from old times. We have to keep moving to the future."[40]

So, with the money Crystal got from her mother for Christmas, Crystal and Traceleen spend the afternoon at a day spa. The very next day after this rejuvenating treatment, Crystal's cousin Shelby comes to town to stay awhile; she brings an assortment of problems into the household, but "once again," as Traceleen relates, "Crystal and I had turned chaos into Zen. Many people have laughed at us for our many years of yoga training and Zen Buddhist retreats, but the strength that had been given us had paid off for many people who come within our circle of attention."[41] In the midst of all this,

Traceleen's niece, with whom she is very close, announces she is pregnant, and she and the baby's father are getting married the next weekend.

In a statement that is actually the point of the story, Traceleen comments "Just when Crystal and I had decided our best days were over, it seems we were being called back into action every time the phone rings."[42] Because now Crystal's daughter-in-law, Jessie, calls to share her news: *she* is pregnant again. The story ends with a sweet sentiment as Traceleen wraps things up this way: "Crystal and I have made New Year's resolutions in February. We have pledged to live our lives to the fullest while we wait to be called back into action in the lives of the young."[43]

This story, then, is a warm, humorous, affirming take on the collection's connecting theme of life's renewal. But it is not an indelible one, not etched in deep lines resulting in an acutely felt picture. The story is easy to enjoy and equally easy to forget; the problem is, it seems a retread of old material— of old recurrent characters who have nothing left of real importance to say to us or to even entertain us very well. Pleasant, unoffending, but certainly not provocative: Gilchrist lite (or, actually, Traceleen lite).

Chapter 10

Ellen Gilchrist's Contribution and Further Evidence of Her Talent (*Collected Stories* and *I, Rhoda Manning, Go Hunting with My Daddy*)

GILCHRIST'S NEXT BOOK, however, erases from memory the relatively weak note upon which the previous short story collection ended. What came next was the *Collected Stories,* appearing in 2000, to considerable—and deserved—acclaim. A "collected stories" step for living authors is impressive, signifying that tribute is being paid to their achievement in the field even before their writing career is over, identifying that particular short story writer as a master. And in Gilchrist's case, the critics as well as the reading public could only concur with her publisher's granting of this honor, with her publisher's estimation of her topflight status as a contemporary short story writer. For instance, in the *New York Times Book Review,* Katherine Dieckmann wrote, "Few writers are as adept at spinning funny, slyly insightful takes that radiate outward like tiny satellites, orbiting a fictional universe that mirrors the more unpredictable and tellingly human moments in our own."[1]

Thirty-four stories were selected for inclusion in her *Collected Stories,* drawn from each of her collections, with the exception of the collection that appeared immediately before, *The Cabal and Other Stories.* A discussion among critics and Gilchrist's loyal fans could go on endlessly about which stories of hers should have been included and which of the ones that are here should not be; but, of course, what this means is that this compilation is no different from any other career-spanning selection—assortment—of any short story writer's output. Quibbling about what stories should have been put in or left out can not distract, however, from appreciating that this *Collected Stories* fulfills the "duty" it should fulfill: a monument to the fact that Gilchrist's work in the short story is her best work; and that, even though all the stories found here deserve loud praise, the ones charting the development of her recurrent female characters represent her most creative, significant, and lasting accomplishment within the form: Rhoda, Nora Jane, Traceleen, Crystal—the "fab four" of Gilchrist's recurrent women. Her absolute masterpiece, "Some Blue Hills at Sundown" (from *Light Can Be Both Wave and Particle*), about Rhoda as a teenager, is correctly included here. The unforgettable debut of Nora Jane in "The Famous Poll at Jody's Bar" reminds us how mature and accomplished Gilchrist presented herself upon *her* debut in her first short story collection, *In the Land of Dreamy Dreams*. Other Nora Jane stories reaffirm our stand that Nora Jane's husband, Freddy Harwood, is Gilchrist's best-drawn male character, lending truth and accuracy to the cliché term *hero*. These stories include "Perhaps a Miracle," "Lunch at the Best Restaurant in the World," and "The Brown Cape," all from *The Courts of Love*.

"Anna, Part I" (from *Drunk with Love*) is the most convincing piece about another recurrent character (but less recurrent than the "big four"), writer Anna Hand. As we indicated in an earlier chapter, this story has all the effectiveness that the novel about Anna Hand, *The Anna Papers,* failed to achieve. The story is the sheer essence of Anna's character, whereas the novel spent too much time with issues that were not strictly Anna's.

But, importantly, such stories as "There's a Garden of Eden" and "In the Land of Dreamy Dreams" (both from the collection *In the Land of Dreamy Dreams*) serve as reminders that, even in writing outside the domains of her recurrent characters, Gilchrist maintains brilliant command of the form. She does not need the comfort of an old-friend character to bring us her findings as she mines her universe for social and familial situations to get at the heart of. On the literary landscape of the U.S., that which highlights work done in the short story, Gilchrist established her corner of it with the publication of her first collection; and that corner of the map she right away claimed as hers has been increasing in size and quality with the publication of each succeeding collection. Her *Collected Stories* made her one of the biggest states on that map, colored in red to be easily noticed and taken for the importance it signifies. As

Library Journal insisted to its librarian subscribers, "this book belongs in every library."[2]

But there is a downside to a living author's being accorded the privilege of am edition of collected stories. Over any subsequent collection automatically hangs the double-edged question, "Oh, are you still writing, and are you still as good as you were?" The stories in any later collection are bound to be judged as evidence of either growth or slippage. Gilchrist's last book to date, *I, Rhoda Manning, Go Hunting with My Daddy* (2002), a story collection, answers the question with: Some are as good as the ones found in her *Collected Stories,* and some are not; and that situation is predictably natural.

As the title of this most recent collection indicates, Gilchrist's most frequently appearing recurrent character is heavily featured. But Rhoda does not step through the pages of all of the stories here; other recurrent characters include Nora Jane; Traceleen and her employer and partner in high jinks, Crystal; interestingly, Amanda McCamey, the protagonist of Gilchrist's first novel, *The Annunciation,* bounces back for another performance. But Rhoda is the dominant presence; the five Rhoda stories (out of a total of 10 stories) form an interlocking sequence that frames Rhoda, now in her sixties, with sons in early middle age and grandchildren in troublesome adolescence. It is an important sequence in the development of the Rhoda Manning character; both individually and collectively, the five Rhoda stories are powerful and resonant investigations into her middle age. Rhoda's personal concerns at this point in her life—while specific to the colorful and even adventuresome life Rhoda has led—nevertheless open out into a broad relevance to anyone having achieved six decades.

The theme of death, or, more specifically, how life arises Phoenix-like from the ashes of death, which was the general thematic underpinning of the previous collection, *The Cabal and Other Stories,* is carried over into this collection as well. But here that theme is developed, of course, specific to Rhoda's life. The death of her father, or his impending death in some of the stories, is the big, looming, overriding situation that is felt, reacted to, analyzed, and lamented in the entire sequence. Her father's life and attitude hang like a cloud—dark one minute, radiant another—over all the Rhoda stories here.

Rhoda's love-hate relationship with her father, her need for his approval and her concomitant need to defy him stamps—defines—all of her subsequent relationships with men, as readers who have been familiar with the Rhoda stories and novels have experienced. From the stories of her childhood in southern Illinois and Indiana during World War II, where her father brought his family so he could do civilian war work, through the stories of her troubled young womanhood with sons and abortions, to these stories of her advent into late middle-age, now with elderly parents, the dominating influence of her father continues. Indeed, Gilchrist's only Rhoda novel to date, *Net of Jewels,* cast in the first person, begins with Rhoda's explaining his narcissism ("a vain and beautiful man who thinks of his children as extensions of his personality").[3]

Obviously from these stories, her obsession with him has never been laid to rest. Now, as a grown woman with grandchildren, how he feels about her and the indelible mark he has made on her life are still being worked out. Four of the five Rhoda stories are told in the first-person, and never before, up to this point in her career, has Gilchrist "sounded" more autobiographical. These stories, the four first-person ones anyway, have a very distinct tone of memoir, or at least of personal essay. Perhaps that "feel" comes from a poignant, appropriate, and actually attractive heartfeltness with which these stories are imbued. The one Rhoda novel, *Net of Jewels,* is the place up to this point where Rhoda is the most meaningfully understood, and her selfishness and egotism not only bearable but actually compelling. Now, in these middle-age-Rhoda stories, a softened Rhoda emerges—the graying of Rhoda—a Rhoda who doesn't need to be constantly and incessantly sexy and competitive and self-centered. She has grown to roundedness—which does not mean, of course, her waistline (she is very weight conscious and fit so that that won't become a problem), but that she has learned to spread her consideration to other people's needs and not dwell simply and exclusively on her own wants and desires. Rhoda readers can step very close to an agreeable protagonist they can easily care about.

So then, in the first story in the collection, the title story, Rhoda is a little girl; but the story is being recalled by the adult Rhoda—that fact made clear in a "postscript." As the stories featuring the girl Rhoda generally have been, this one is set in southern Illinois during World War II, where her father is "building levees on the Mississippi River" as "chief engineer for the Louisville District of the Corps of Engineers."[4] And as is often the case in the girl-Rhoda stories, her oldest brother, Dudley, is a presence, both as a threat and as an object of her envy. The premise of this story is Rhoda's persistence in wanting to go hunting with her daddy and Dudley; finally she succeeds in being invited to join a hunting party. In a typical Rhoda assertion, she remembers that "I was five and a half years old and I could think and plan as well as I could when I was thirty." And this, too: "If there was something I wanted, I was after it until it was mine."[5]

She has only a BB gun on this hunting expedition, but even with such limited firepower she makes a careless mistake in terms of hunting safety; but she has lost interest in the endeavor anyway—"hunting was turning out to be a lot like a lot of other things they thought up to do. A lot of work for nothing."[6] And that is what her hunting venture amounted to; but in the "postscript," the adult Rhoda posits that the real gist of her hunting trip was how wonderful a man her father was. "I wouldn't want to miss this opportunity to tell you what it's like to go hunting with a man who would kill or die for you. A strong man that other men seek out and love. It's a gift for a girl to have that kind of father and it's also a curse. It's a gift because you have a safe and fortunate childhood and can grow up strong and unafraid. It's a curse because you cannot reproduce it in the adult world. No man can be that wonderful ever again because only a child's mind can really comprehend wonder."[7]

And thus is established the bridge between all the Rhoda stories in the sequence: the adoration of her father and the realization, once he is gone, that she had loved him more than anyone else. But the corollary to the major theme here of the dominant role her father has played in her life is "the male thing": the exclusivity of the males in her family, a club including her father, her brothers, and, when she has them and they arrive into adolescence, her three sons. From the time she was a child, Rhoda has realized her inferior status in the family because of her gender. (She refers to her brother Dudley here in this story as in possession of a "privileged position as the oldest male heir.")[8] And of course her mother offers Rhoda no role model in terms of how to gain acceptance into the club or at least how to grow strong and independent on one's own outside the club. Mrs. Manning is drawn in "I, Rhoda Manning, Go Hunting with My Daddy" exactly as she has been depicted in previous Rhoda stories: the traditional, supportive rather than active southern housewife ("She was from the Delta and liked to dress up and have servants and practice French and go to the Episcopal church. She didn't like to go outside and get her shoes dirty and have any bug bites on her.")[9]

The third level of thematic connection here in these Rhoda stories—the first being her love/obsession with her father, the second her exclusion even as an adult from the male club her father and brothers and even her own sons make up—is the overt control her father attempts to assert over her sons. Granted, in adolescence and in their teenage years, Rhoda had lost control of them; and they fell victim to the epidemic sweeping the world of the young at the end of the twentieth century: drug use. At the same time that Rhoda's father has become aware of his grandsons' problems—more aware and determined to do something about it than the denial-prone Rhoda—he has also gotten increasingly closed minded in a social sense, even to the point of bigotry. The South he used to love he now finds decadent, and he moves himself and Rhoda's mother to the pristine—and overwhelmingly *white*—loveliness of Wyoming. (Although in the story "On the Wind River in Wyoming" Rhoda's mother finally asserts herself, having had enough of simply following her husband through life, and she moves back eastward to New Orleans; Rhoda's father, meanwhile, installs a girlfriend in his house in Wyoming.) Since he can't seem to lure his children out to join him in the good, clean air of the Rockies, to lead a good, clean life, he persists in handling Rhoda's difficult sons with tough love. "He loved my sons with [a] passion and had been plotting for years to take them away from me," Rhoda avers.[10]

So, in the sequence of Rhoda stories presented here, "I, Rhoda Manning, Go Hunting with My Daddy," "Entropy," "A Christmas in Wyoming," "On the Wind River in Wyoming," and "The Golden Bough," Rhoda lives as if under a mountain—the mountain being her father, of course. She feels as if she is simply a genetic bridge between her father and her sons. But in these closing years of her father's life, and after his death, Rhoda is proud that, "after twenty-four years of psychotherapy and four years of recovering from psychotherapy . . . I realized how much I loved the man. I was him. I was more like him than either of my brothers. If I stopped loving him I would have to stop loving the most powerful parts of myself."[11] As far as the more biological side of what she inherited from him and passed on to her sons, Rhoda accepts that "his influence on all of us and the genes he gave us may be a mixed blessing but I don't know anyone in my family who wants to give any of it back or change it for any other influence or set of genes."[12]

The story "Gotterdammerung, in which Nora Jane and Freddy Harwood Confront Evil in a World They Never Made" is not simply the reappearance of another prominent recurrent character, Nora Jane Whittington, but is, more specifically, a continuation and sequel to a previous Nora Jane story, "On the Problem of Turbulence" from the collection *The Courts of Love*. That previous story, as does this one, concerned violent terrorist activity carried out in the U.S. by Islamic fundamentalists—in this case, a sect reacting against Indian writer Salmon Rushdie and the publishers and booksellers who traffic in his work. It should not be forgotten, then, that Nora Jane's husband Freddy owns a bookstore in Berkeley, California, and the plot of the previous story, "On the Problem of Turbulence," in what amounts to a two-part sequence was this: In San Francisco, the sect mistakenly murdered the girlfriend of the famous American publisher of Rushdie; they had intended to kill *him,* not her. And they bombed Freddy's store for featuring Rushdie's books. Now, in this story "Gotterdammerung," Freddy remains on their hit list, and he and the others on the list are to be killed as revenge—now some years after the fact—for the men who killed the girlfriend being sent to prison.

The story actually begins in New York City, where the fellow co-op owners of a building on the Upper East Side are upset over the carryings-on in one of the units. "In late July of 2000, several tall, unpleasant-looking Middle Eastern men began to leave and enter the apartment at all hours of the day and night and the music began to blare out of the open windows."[13] (In an "Author's Note" at the beginning of the book, Gilchrist insists that she is not "prescient" vis-à-vis September 11, 2001.) When a co-op busybody surreptitiously enters the offending apartment and finds the hit list, the list is turned over to the FBI; and the "action" now switches to Berkeley, where Nora Jane receives an invitation to sing at a benefit for the Planned Parenthood organization at the Metropolitan Opera House in New York (the plot, granted, stretches a little thin in credibility right at this point).

Nora Jane is hesitant to accept. But in the end she relents and agrees to do it. In the meantime, the sect's killer journeys to California to dispatch Freddy. Unbeknown to that group *or* to Freddy and Nora Jane, the FBI has also sent a team of their own to protect Freddy from his anonymous enemies. No harm comes to Freddy, and a mountain lion he has somewhat "befriended," who lives in the vicinity of his house in the mountains outside Berkeley, helps in the defeat of the terrorists—an inadvertent circumstance, really, not in some sort of Lassie-to-the-rescue kind of situation.

This story grips the reader: Gilchrist ventures into the thriller genre, and it works. And in terms of making things work, the next story, "The Abortion," demonstrates how Gilchrist has learned to use one of her often annoying technical traits to a story's advantage. For this story Gilchrist has brought back the main character of her first novel, *The Annunciation,* writer and scholar Amanda McCamey. Amanda has actually appeared on a couple occasions since that novel, in the stories "The Song of Songs" and "Life on the Earth," both in the collection *Light Can Be Both Wave and Particle.* Here, now, Amanda and her husband Will have a teenage son, whom they adore, and who has impregnated his equally young girlfriend. As the story progresses, the point of view moves back and forth and around from Amanda to Will to their son to his girlfriend to the doctor who performs the abortion on her—that is, moves smoothly and appropriately, not jarringly within the same paragraph. This prevents sending the reader down little blind alleys away from the main story line. Here the opposite is true: the shifts all contribute to the story's effectiveness as a deeply felt take on the difficult passage into adulthood—this take emphasizing how the transition can be eased by loving parents.

The last story in the collection, "Light Shining Through a Honey Jar," features that dynamic duo Crystal Manning of New Orleans and her black maid, the wise and devoted sidekick, Traceleen. It certainly is not the best story about these two recurrent characters, but it holds reader attention as the boyfriend of the new nanny for Traceleen's beloved little grandnieces goes on a drug-induced berserk episode and holds the nanny and the little girls hostage. No one is hurt and things get back to order in Traceleen and Crystal's world—giving further evidence of Traceleen's abilities at peace keeping. This story, jolting in plot situation but comfortably predictable in its presentation of the superb qualities of the wonderful Traceleen, is a fitting way to finish reading all of Gilchrist's works so far. This volume ends, virtually, in ellipses. . . . More of her recurrent characters to come. . . .

Conclusion

ELLEN GILCHRIST'S REPUTATION as a fiction writer rests primarily—rightfully—on her distinctive, realistic, indefatigable female characters. With a cat's eye—an eye exquisitely sensitive to any motion within its line of vision—she catches a characters' every movement. But the talent of that kind of acute sensitivity—a talent that is indeed Gilchrist's—is relating to the reader only the *significant* movements that tell most about these characters. As we have seen, Gilchrist is a master of the brief but telling and resonant description/definition of a character; the thumbnail sketch becomes an art form unto itself in her hands.

After all is said and done, after all her work is read and thought about, her major theme steps to the fore as *unhappiness*—unhappiness often taking the form of loneliness. Initially the reader gathers that Gilchrist's overriding theme is just what she is known for: the strength women can have in hand, are sometimes ambivalent about, and will either suffer or enjoy the consequences of exerting. In the full extent of her fiction, though, in the reading of all her books in order, the *actual* thematic underpinning and interconnection rises to the surface: *unhappiness*. Beneath her female characters' displays of strength lies the truth that strength is derived from facing, and facing down, unhappiness. Stepping out of the mire of unhappiness, learning to avoid it in the first place, is the origin of their strength; and finding relief from it, or circumventing it altogether, is what leads Gilchrist's female characters to need love, to be loved but also *to love*. The steps they take from their personal unhappiness, especially loneliness, to arrive at love are really what her novels and short stories are about; and, of course, these paths are fraught with ambivalence, indecisiveness, successes and, as many times, failures. Thus is the fundamental reason for her fiction's appeal: its familiarity. Essentially, what her characters go through, we *all* have gone through.

Gilchrist's oeuvre strikes the reader who is fortunate enough to have completed every volume of it as primarily a web of interconnectedness, the threads being her recurrent characters. The best of her recurrent characters are unmistakable personalities: distinct, vibrant, profoundly realized, entertaining, and *honest* characters. That they also *evolve* as characters—not only aging but also undergoing personality development as the stories continue to appear over the years—is not only a testament to their grounding in *real* behavior but also to the dividend power of recurrent characters to readers who have been following Gilchrist's work all along. It is as if she is aware of—having planned it this way, in fact—that the biggest payoff of her fiction is to the reader whom she attracted at the beginning and has been loyal to her ever since. The return of the best of her recurrent characters—Rhoda, Nora Jane, Crystal, Traceleen—to the stage time and again permits more occasions to illuminate further facets of their personality.

As we have witnessed, though, there are drawbacks to the heavy use of recurrent characters. Most notably, the Hand family, who populate, it will be recalled, the novels *The Anna Papers* and *Starcarbon* and the trio of novellas collected in *I Cannot Get You Close Enough*. The lesson learned from the Hands is that characters that are thin to begin with can be stretched to tenuity when made to recur too often. Stretched not to sheerness of who they are but to the point of insubstantiality. But, in this matter as in all matters regarding the estimation of an author's whole output, the bigger picture is of primary importance, and the bigger picture here is how amazingly fresh, generally speaking, Gilchrist keeps her recurrent characters, the Hands notwithstanding. We have seen *how* this happens, when Gilchrist causes it to happen: She creates new, provocative situations in which the characters are placed, and thus different angles of their personalities are able to shine, like a delicately cut gem, but all these angles centered on, grounded in, the original concept of the character.

The best of the best of her recurrent characters are the child Rhoda and Nora Jane; and the stories of Rhoda as a little girl and *all* the Nora Jane stories are Gilchrist's greatest achievement, her most resonant work, because Nora Jane and the child Rhoda are her most honestly realized characters and the most compelling to read about. They are the most likable of them all. And when given a choice, readers will gravitate more readily to likable characters. Does being likable make characters better—or, rather, does it mean the *characterizations* are *done* better? Not necessarily, of course; not necessarily as a rule of fiction writing. But in Gilchrist's case—when weighing the merits of one of her recurrent female protagonists against another—the answer is, Yes. These characterizations *are* done better. So much of Gilchrist's appeal stems from how well she communicates with her reader *by way of* her distinctive characters, and more of what she has to say about life and love and the necessity of the former being full of the latter will be listened to by her readers responding to *likable* characters. They are pleasant to be around; they are aggravating in their less than noble moments, yes, but that only renders their likability truer to the way people actually are and thus gives them full acceptability *as* characters.

The insistence upon the superiority of the stories about Nora Jane and the child Rhoda can only lead to making a greater insistence: that Gilchrist is, generally speaking, a more effective short story writer than novelist. Her chronic point of view problems in her short story work, much cited in previous pages as we progressed through her oeuvre, nevertheless are seen, in standing back to for a broader view, as only minor impediments—minor irritations—in the ultimate appreciation of the pinpoint distillation that defines her short stories. To set characters down and let them go far is the benefit of the novel. To *suggest* where they have been and to *imply* where they will go next is the requirement of the short story. Gilchrist is best at the suggestion and implication (facilitated, of course, by her limpid, precise, sheerly eloquent writing style). More of her short stories show this ability than her novels show an authoritative command of extending the frame to give bigger accounts of the lives created for her characters.

Of course, the positive qualities of Gilchrist's fiction can not be spoken about without referring also to her exemplary use of dialogue as a tool—a device—for concisely developing depths and sides to characters and advancing the plot. The reader's unconsciousness of the process is, of course, the talent of it—again, a talent Gilchrist unstintingly demonstrates. Also, it must be given full credit that even with the admirable and effective concision of her dialogue, her characters do not sound alike, a practice that Gilchrist accomplishes with such subtlety it must be second nature with her; and the very subtlety of it, of course, ensures its greatest effectiveness and least obtrusiveness.

Gilchrist writes from the heart. She is no chemist. Her creative employ of characters, and the dynamic and telling familial and social situations into which she places them, is not done as a laboratory experiment for cold analysis and breakdown of the component parts of their reactions. But done for the reader to *feel* where her characters' passions lead them. She eschews deep examinations through an intellectual and intellectualizing prism in favor of letting characters let their *own* hearts dictate paths taken, uphill and down, to safe places and places not so safe.

It is not my intention, but at the same time I suspect it is not my effect, to end this conclusion and thus the whole book on a negative note; but let us address the question of Gilchrist's "vision"—i.e. her personal view of the social order as it is and as it should be. The necessary point to make about her vision is that she really does not have one—a statement requiring immediate follow-up by the insistence that she does not *need* one. She presents no great pattern of understanding when it comes to the human condition, she possesses no great picture of life that she insists on building on with each book; but she does not *need* one. She owns no grand view of existence that is hers and hers alone and that each book gives further expression to; simply because does not *need* one. Her oeuvre is based on instinct—about the power of love, as simple as that sounds. Granted, that perhaps constitutes a vision of sorts; but, really, it translates more as a guiding light than an actual vision, a light shining on each sentence as she writes it, to keep reminding her of the power of love. And, further, a light that attracts a sympathetic readership. Her appeal to her considerable readership is that her works are *not* saddled with any "big picture" that stretches beyond the boundaries of readers' own experiences and interests. Gilchrist offers no uniquely "smart" way of regarding life; but what she *does* offer is a clear, humorous, poignant, *honest* way of seeing the familiar world that we all inhabit: a world governed by love. Her lens for viewing this world is, simply, her heart.

Notes

Chapter 1

1. *Sarah Conley.* 1997. Little, Brown. pp. 74.
2. *Sarah Conley.* p. 94.
3. *Falling Through Space: The Journals of Ellen Gilchrist.* 1987. University Press of Mississippi. p. 94.
4. Ibid. p. 213.
5. Carol Shields. *Jane Austen.* 2001. Viking. p. 10.
6. *Dictionary of Literary Biography.* Vol. 130: American Short-Story Writers Since World War II. 1993. pp. 178–87.
7. Ibid.
8. Ibid.
9. *Contemporary Novelists*, 4th ed. Ed. D.L. Kirkpatrick. 1986. St. Martin's. pp. 338–9.
10. *Dictionary of Literary Biography.* pp. 178–87.
11. *A Reader's Guide to Twentieth-Century Writers.* Ed. Peter Parker. 1966. Oxford. pp. 272–3.
12. *Contemporary Novelists*, pp. 338–9.
13. Ibid.

Chapter 2

1. Jim Crace. *Times Literary Supplement.* No. 4150. Oct. 15, 1982. p. 1142.
2. Jeanie Thompson and Anita Miller Garner. "The Miracle of Realism: The Bid for Self-Knowledge in the Fiction of Ellen Gilchrist." *The Southern Quarterly.* Vol. 22. No. 1, Fall 1983. pp. 104–14.

3. Dorie Larue. "Progress and Prescription: Ellen Gilchrist's Southern Belles." *The Southern Quarterly.* Vol. 31. No. 3. Spring 1993. pp. 69–78.

4. *Contemporary Novelists*, 4th ed. Ed. D.L. Kirkpatrick. 1986. St. Martin's. p. 338.

5. *Falling Through Space.* 1987. University Press of Mississippi. p. 108.

6. Ibid. p. 152.

7. Ibid. p. 153.

8. Ibid. p. 155.

9. *In the Land of Dreamy Dreams.* 2002. Louisiana State University Press. p. 3.

10. Ibid. p. 3

11. Ibid.

12. Ibid.

13. Ibid. p. 4.

14. Ibid. p. 7.

15. Ibid.

16. Ibid.

17. Ibid. p. 8.

18. Ibid.

19. Ibid.

20. Ibid.

21. Ibid.

22. Ibid. p. 9.

23. Ibid.

24. Ibid.

25. Ibid.

26. Ibid. p. 10.

27. Ibid. p. 11.

28. Ibid. p. 13.

29. Ibid. p. 16.

30. Ibid. p. 17.

31. Ibid.

32. Ibid.

33. Ibid. p. 23.

34. *Falling Through Space.* p. 126.

35. *In the Land of Dreamy Dreams.* p. 81.

36. Ibid. p. 82.

37. Ibid. p. 84.

38. Ibid.

39. Ibid. p. 86.

40. Ibid. p. 92.
41. Ibid. p. 93.
42. Ibid. p. 95.
43. Ibid. p. 111.
44. Ibid.
45. Ibid. p. 112.
46. Ibid. p. 113.
47. Ibid. pp. 114–5.
48. Ibid. p. 115.
49. Ibid. p. 123.
50. Ibid. p. 124.
51. Ibid. p. 125.
52. Ibid. p. 126.
53. Ibid. p. 130.
54. Ibid. p. 131.
55. Ibid. p. 133.
56. Ibid. pp. 136–7.
57. Ibid. p. 49.
58. Ibid.
59. Ibid. p. 50.
60. Ibid. p. 52.
61. Ibid. p. 59.
62. Ibid.

Chapter 3

1. *The Annunciation*. 2001. Louisiana State University Press. p. 6.
2. Ibid. p. 12.
3. Ibid. p. 20.
4. Ibid. p. 32.
5. Ibid. p. 47.
6. Ibid.
7. Ibid.
8. Ibid. p. 46.
9. Ibid. p. 50.
10. Ibid. p. 58.
11. Ibid. p. 59.
12. Ibid. p. 117.
13. Ibid. p. 119.
14. Ibid. p. 127.
15. Ibid. p. 135.

16. Ibid. p. 141.
17. Ibid. p. 147.
18. Ibid. p. 151.
19. Ibid. p. 189.
20. Ibid.
21. Ibid. p. 279.
22. Ibid. p. 284.
23. Ibid. pp. 292–3.
24. Ibid. p. 333.
25. Frances Taliaferro. *Harper's*. Vol. 266. June, 1983. p. 76.
26. Rosellen Brown. *Saturday Review*. Vol. 9. July/August 1983. p. 53.
27. Jonathan Yardley, "Knockout Victory: The Best Stories Yet from Ellen Gilchrist." *Washington Post*. Sept. 12, 1984. p. BI.

Chapter 4

1. David Sexton. *Times Literary Supplement*. May 24, 1988. p. 573.
2. Jonathan Yardley. *Washington Post*, p. BI.
3. *Victory over Japan.* 1984. Little Brown/Back Bay. p. 4.
4. Ibid. pp. 4-5.
5. Ibid. p. 7.
6. Ibid. pp. 7–8.
7. Ibid. p. 11.
8. Ibid.
9. Ibid. p. 15.
10. Ibid.
11. Ibid. p. 17.
12. Ibid. p. 19.
13. Ibid. p. 38.
14. Ibid.
15. Ibid. p. 39.
16. Ibid. p. 53.
17. Ibid. p. 56.
18. Ibid. p. 68.
19. Ibid. p. 63.
20. *Drunk with Love.* 1986. Little, Brown. p. 29.
21. Ibid.
22. Ibid. p. 31.
23. Ibid. p. 33.
24. Ibid.

25. Ibid. p. 35.
26. Ibid. p. 36.
27. Ibid. p. 37.
28. Ibid. p. 41.
29. Ibid. p. 49.
30. Ibid. p. 52.
31. Ibid.
32. Ibid. p. 56.
33. Ibid. p. 60.
34. Ibid. p. 61.
35. Ibid. p. 62.
36. Ibid. p. 64.
37. *Victory over Japan.* p. 148.
38. Ibid. p. 151.
39. Ibid. p. 153.
40. Ibid. p. 154.
41. Ibid. p. 158.
42. Ibid. p. 167.
43. Ibid. p. 168.
44. Ibid. p. 174.
45. Ibid. p. 187.
46. Ibid. p. 192.
47. Ibid. p. 194.
48. Ibid. p. 195.
49. *Drunk with Love.* p. 13.
50. Ibid.
51. Ibid. p. 17.
52. Ibid. p. 19.
53. Ibid. p. 20.
54. Ibid. pp. 24-5.
55. *Victory over Japan.* p. 207.
56. Ibid. p. 211.
57. Ibid. p. 212.
58. Ibid.
59. Ibid. p. 215.
60. Ibid. p. 221.
61. Ibid. p. 224.
62. Ibid. p. 225.
63. Ibid. p. 231.
64. *Drunk with Love.* p. 203.

65. *Victory over Japan.* p. 96.
66. Ibid. p. 102.
67. Ibid. p. 110.
68. Meg Wolitzer. *Los Angeles Times Book Review.* Sept. 14, 1986. pp. 2,12.
69. John Seabrook. *Christian Science Monitor.* Dec. 7, 1984. p. 38.

Chapter 5

1. *Victory over Japan.* p. 75.
2. Ibid. p. 89.
3. Ibid. p. 93.
4. Ibid. p. 95.
5. *Drunk with Love.* p. 221.
6. Ibid. p. 225.
7. Ibid. p. 229.
8. Ibid. p. 231.
9. Ibid. p. 231.
10. *The Anna Papers.* 1998. Little, Brown. p. 49.
11. Ibid. p. 114.
12. Ibid. p. 115.
13. Ibid. p. 116.
14. Ibid. p. 149.
15. *I Cannot Get You Close Enough.* Little, Brown. p. 3.
16. Ibid. p. 31.
17. Ibid. p. 89.
18. Ibid. p. 90.
19. Ibid. p. 91.
20. Ibid. p. 197.
21. Ibid. p. 242.
22. Ibid. p. 241.
23. Anna Vaux. "Spoilt Southerners." *Time Literary Supplement.* No. 4626. Nov. 29, 1991. p. 22.

Chapter 6

1. *Light Can Be Both Wave and Particle.* 1989. Little, Brown/Back Bay. p. 26.
2. Ibid.
3. Ibid. p. 27.
4. Ibid.

5. Ibid. pp. 27-8.
6. Ibid. p. 28.
7. Ibid. p. 29.
8. Ibid. pp. 29–30.
9. Ibid. p. 30.
10. Larue, Dorie. "Progress and Prescription." p. 78.
11. *Light Can Be Both Wave and Particle.* p. 115.
12. Ibid. p. 118.
13. Ibid. p. 125.
14. Ibid. p. 133.
15. Ibid. p. 39.
16. Ibid. p. 44.
17. Ibid. p. 59.
18. Ibid. p. 67.
19. Ibid. p. 69.
20. Ibid. p. 83.
21. Ibid. p. 92.
22. Paul Stuewe, *Quill & Quire.* No.55, Dec. 1989, p. 29.
23. *Publisher's Weekly.* Aug. 4, 1989.

Chapter 7

1. *Net of Jewels.* 1992. Little, Brown. p. 3.
2. Ibid. p. 11.
3. Ibid. p. 31.
4. Ibid. p. 237.
5. Ibid. p. 236.
6. Ibid. p. 247.
7. Ibid. p. 3.
8. Lorna Stage. "Fleeing from Daddy." *Times Literary Supplement.* No. 4689. Feb. 12, 1993. p. 22.
9. Dorie Larue. "Progress and Prescription," p. 69.
10. *Publisher's Weekly.* Jan. 31, 1994.
11. *Anabasis.* 1995. University Press of Mississippi, p. 164.
12. Ibid. p. 97.
13. Ibid. preface (no page number)
14. Ibid. p. 3.
15. Ibid. p. 24.
16. Ibid. p. 34.
17. Ibid. p. 38.

18. Ibid. p. 48.
19. Ibid. p. 52.
20. Ibid.
21. Ibid. p. 95.
22. Ibid. p. 108.
23. Ibid. p. 109.
24. Ibid. p. 122.
25. Ibid. p. 211.
26. Ibid. p. 46.
27. Ibid. p. 59.
28. Ibid. p. 96.
29. Margaret A. Robinson. *New York Times Book Review.* Oct. 30, 1994. p. 48.
30. *Kirkus Reviews.* July 1, 1994.

Chapter 8

1. *The Age of Miracles.* 1995. Little, Brown, p. 4.
2. Ibid. p. 245.
3. Ibid. p. 147.
4. Ibid. p. 54.
5. Ibid. p. 58.
6. Ibid. p. 65.
7. Ibid. p. 19.
8. Ibid. p. 46.
9. Ibid. p. 36.
10. Julie Glass. "The Rough-Edged Romantic." *Chicago Tribune.* June 11, 1995. p. 6.
11. *Rhoda: A Life in Stories.* 1995. Little, Brown/Back Bay. p. vii.
12. Ibid. p. viii.
13. Ibid. p. ix.
14. Ibid. p. 77.
15. Ibid. p. 87.
16. Ibid. p. 77.
17. Ibid. p. 230.
18. Ibid.
19. Ibid. p. 230.
20. *The Courts of Love.* 1997. Little, Brown/Back Bay. p. 9.
21. Ibid. p. 12.
22. Ibid. p. 19.

23. Ibid. p. 22.
24. Ibid. p. 36.
25. Ibid. p. 38.
26. Ibid. p. 39.
27. Ibid. p. 43.
28. Ibid. p. 41.
29. Ibid. p. 1.
30. Ibid.
31. Ibid. p. 90.
32. Ibid. p. 134.
33. Ibid. p. 144.
34. Ibid. pp. 145-6.
35. Ibid. p. 227.
36. Ibid. p. 249.
37. Ibid. p. 250.
38. Ibid.
39. Ibid. p. 268.
40. *Sarah Conley.* p. 9.
41. Ibid. p. 21.
42. Ibid. p. 24.
43. Ibid. p. 26.
44. Ibid.
45. Ibid. p. 33.
46. Ibid. p. 34.
47. Ibid. p. 38.
48. Ibid. p. 85.
49. Ibid. p. 62.
50. Ibid. p. 27.
51. Ibid. p. 58.
52. Patrick Giles. *New York Times Book Review,* Nov. 9, 1997. p. 22.
53. Donna Seaman. *Booklist.* Vol. 93, No. 22, Aug. 1, 1997, p. 1846.
54. Margaret Donavin Bauer. *The Fiction of Ellen Gilchrist.* 1999. University Press of Florida. pp. 1–22.

Chapter 9

1. *Flights of Angels.* 1999. Little, Brown/Back Bay. p. 97.
2. Ibid. p. 99.
3. Ibid. pp. 100-01.
4. Ibid. p. 103.

5. Ibid.
6. Ibid. p. 115.
7. Ibid. p. 117.
8. Ibid. p. 73.
9. Ibid. p. 77.
10. Ibid. p. 79.
11. Ibid. p. 78.
12. Ibid. p. 88.
13. Ibid. p. 94.
14. *The Cabal and Other Stories*. 2002. Little, Brown/
    Back Bay, p. 3.
15. Ibid. p. 4.
16. Ibid.
17. Ibid. p. 5.
18. Ibid. p. 6.
19. Ibid. p. 6.
20. Ibid. p. 15.
21. Ibid. p. 43.
22. Ibid. p. 47.
23. Ibid. pp. 50-1.
24. Ibid. p. 53.
25. Ibid. p. 65.
26. Ibid. p. 76.
27. Ibid. p. 80.
28. Ibid. p. 124.
29. Ibid. p. 132.
30. Ibid. p. 140.
31. Ibid. p. 154.
32. Ibid. p. 156.
33. Ibid. p. 166.
34. Ibid. p. 213.
35. Ibid. p. 213.
36. Ibid. p. 214.
37. Ibid. p. 217.
38. Ibid. p. 234.
39. Ibid. p. 243.
40. Ibid. p. 250.
41. Ibid. p. 261.
42. Ibid. p. 268.
43. Ibid. p. 272.

Chapter 10

1. Katherine Dieckmann. *New York Times Book Review.* Vol. 105. No. 51. Dec. 17, 2000. p. 8.
2. Christine DeZelar-Tiedman. *Library Journal.* Vol.125. No. 17. Oct. 15, 2000. p. 107.
3. *Net of Jewels.* p. 3.
4. *I, Rhoda Manning, Go Hunting with My Daddy.* 2002. Little, Brown, p. 3.
5. Ibid. pp. 7–8.
6. Ibid. p. 11.
7. Ibid. p. 18.
8. Ibid. p. 12.
9. Ibid. p. 5.
10. Ibid. p. 83.
11. Ibid. p. 93.
12. Ibid. p. 83.
13. Ibid. p. 136.

Bibliography

Editions of Ellen Gilchrist's Works Cited in Text

The Age of Miracles. 1995. Little, Brown.
Anabasis. 1995. University Press of Mississippi. Paper.
The Anna Papers. 1998. Little, Brown. Paper.
The Annunciation. 2001. Louisiana State University. Paper.
The Cabal and Other Stories. 2002. Little, Brown/Back Bay. Paper.
Collected Stories. 2001. Little, Brown/Back Bay. Paper.
The Courts of Love. 1997. Little Brown/Back. Paper.
Drunk with Love. 1986. Little, Brown. Paper.
Falling through Space: The Journals of Ellen Gilchrist. 1987. University Press of Mississippi. Paper.
Flights of Angels. 1999. Little, Brown/Back Bay. Paper.
I Cannot Get You Close Enough. Little, Brown. Paper.
I, Rhoda Manning, Go Hunting with My Daddy. 2002. Little, Brown.
In the Land of Dreamy Dreams. 2002. Louisiana State University. Paper.
Light Can Be Both Wave and Particle. 1989. Little, Brown/Back Bay. Paper.
Net of Jewels. 1992. Little, Brown.
Rhoda: A Life in Stories. 1995. Little, Brown/Back Bay. Paper.
Sarah Conley. 1998. Little, Brown/Back Bay. Paper.
Starcarbon. 1994. Little, Brown/Back Bay. Paper.
Victory over Japan. 1984. Little, Brown/Back Bay. Paper.

Secondary Sources

Bain, Robert. "Ellen Gilchrist," *Contemporary Fiction Writers of the South: A Bio-Bibliographic Sourcebook.* 1993. Greenwood.

Bauer, Margaret Donavin. *The Fiction of Ellen Gilchrist*. 1999. University Press of Mississippi.

Dictionary of Literary Biography. Vol. 130: American Short-Story Writers Since World War II. 1993. Gale.

Larue, Dorie. "Progress and Prescription: Ellen Gilchrist's Southern Belles," *The Southern Quarterly*. Vol. 31, No. 3, Spring 1993. pp. 69–78.

McKay, Mary A. *Ellen Gilchrist*. 1997. Twayne.

Thompson, Jeanie and Garner, Anita Miller. "The Miracle of Realism: The Bid for Self-Knowledge in the Fiction of Ellen Gilchrist," *The Southern Quarterly*, Vol. 22, No. 1, Fall 1993, pp. 104–14; reprinted in *Women Writers of the Contemporary South*. Ed. by Peggy Prenshaw. 1984. University Press of Mississippi. pp. 233–247.

Index

About the Author

BRAD HOOPER is Adult Books editor for *Booklist Magazine*. He has published several short stories, essays, and reviews in various publications, and he is the author of *The Short Story Reader' Advisory: A Guide to the Best*.